Kingsville Ontario Book 1 in Colour Photos, Saving Our History One Photo at a Time

Photography
by Barbara Raué
2015

Series Name:
Cruising Ontario

Book 123: Kingsville Book 1

Cover photo: 98 Main Street East

Series Name: Cruising Ontario
Saving Our History One Photo at a Time
in colour photos

Books Available in Alphabetical Order:
Aberfoyle, Acton, Alton, Ancaster, Arthur, Aylmer, Ayr,
Bloomingdale, Brantford, Burlington, Caledon, Caledonia,
Cambridge, Clifford, Conestogo, Delhi, Dorchester to Aylmer,
Drayton, Drumbo, Dundas, Eden Mills, Elmira, Elora, Fergus,
Guelph, Hagersville, Hamilton, Hanover, Harriston, Hespeler,
Jarvis, Kitchener, Linwood, Listowel, London, Lucknow,
Mono, Mount Forest, Neustadt, New Hamburg, Niagara-on-
the-Lake, Oakville, Orangeville, Orillia, Owen Sound,
Palmerston, Peterborough, Port Elgin, Preston, Rockwood,
Seaforth, Sheffield, Shelburne, Simcoe, Southampton, St.
Jacobs, St. Thomas, Stoney Creek, Stratford, Tillsonburg,
Waterdown, Waterford, Waterloo, Wellesley, Wingham

Book 110:Lucknow,Mitchell
Book 111: Conestogo, Bloomingdale
Book 112: Delhi
Book 113: Waterford
Book 114-116: Waterloo
Book 117-119: Windsor
Book 120-121: Amherstburg
Book 122: Essex
Book 123-124: Kingsville & Area

Other Books by Barbara Raue

Coins of Gold

Arrows, Indians and Love

The Life and Times of Barbara
Volume 1: Inventions That Have Enhanced My Life
Volume 2: Entertainment That I Have Enjoyed
Volume 3: East Coast Trips
Volume 4: Olympics Have Always Intrigued Me
Volume 5: Wonders of the World
Volume 6: Caribbean Cruises We Have Enjoyed
Volume 7: Animals
Volume 8: Storms and Other Major Disasters in My Lifetime
Volume 9: Wars, Terrorist Attacks and Major Disasters

The Cromwell Family Book

Laura Secord Discovered

Daddy Where Are You?

Visit Barbara's website to view all of her books
http://barbararaue.ca

Kingsville is located in Essex County in southwestern Ontario, west of Leamington, south of Lakeshore, southeast of Essex. It is primarily an agricultural community nestled along the north shore of Lake Erie. The terrain is generally flat, and consists of a mixture of various rocks, sand and clay. The town is about 570 feet above sea level.

Kingsville is home to the Jack Miner Bird Sanctuary. Jack Miner was awarded The Order of the British Empire (OBE) for his achievements in conservation in the British Empire. Jack Miner is considered "the father of the conservation movement on the continent".

The Town of Kingsville is rich in history and Victorian era architecture.

Table of Contents

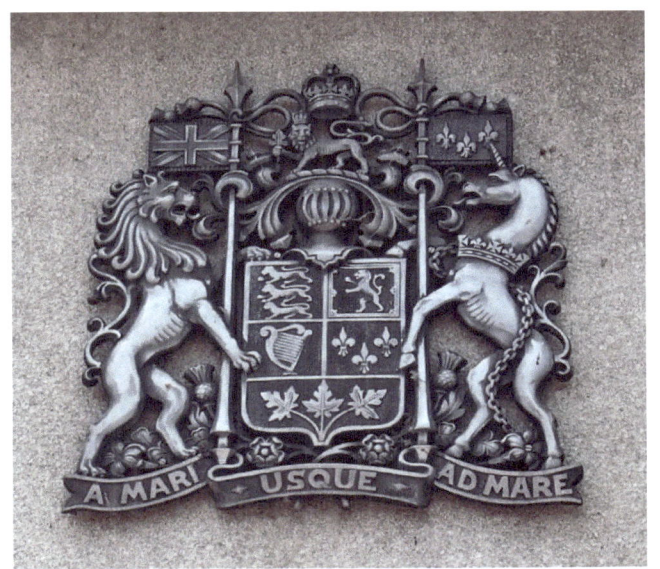

Federal Building crest

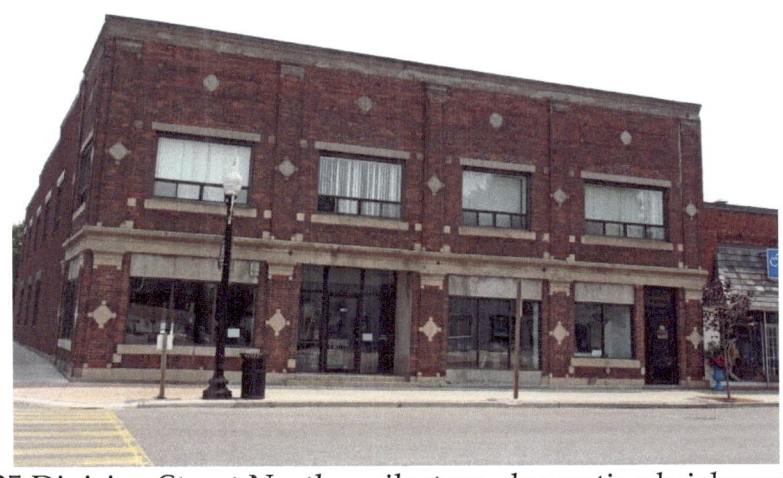

25 Division Street North – pilasters, decorative brickwork

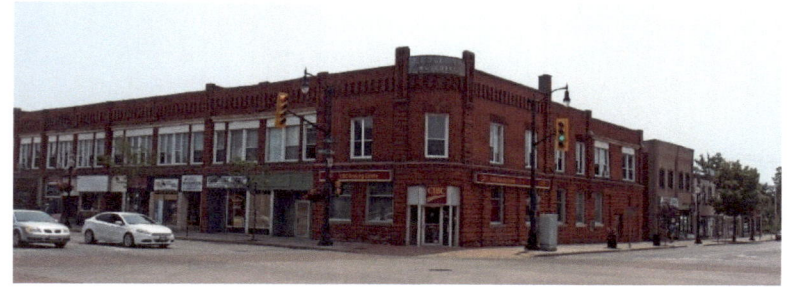

Division and Main Streets corner

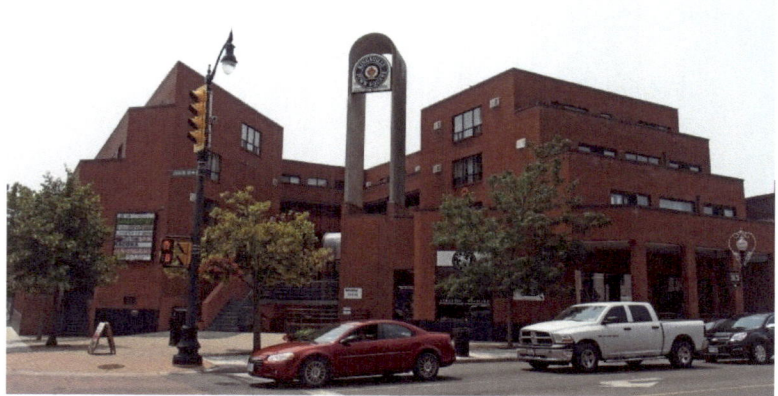

Kingsville Town Square

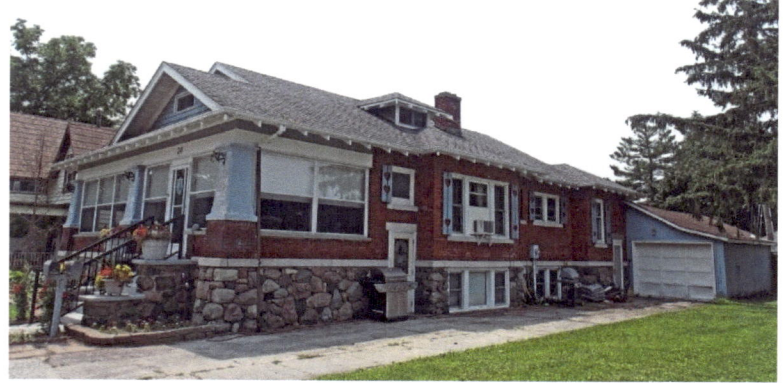

38 Division Street – cobblestone foundation

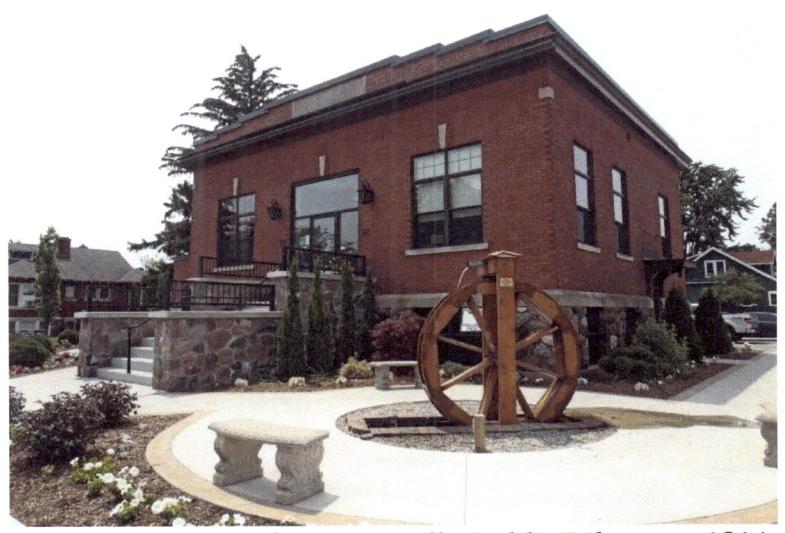

28 Division Street South - Kingsville Public Library – 1914 – single storey, Art Deco style; raised, cut-fieldstone foundation; local Broadwell brick; decorative brick headers with keystones; "soldier courses" of brickwork (bricks laid vertically with long narrow sides exposed); flat roof with stepped parapet

Kingsville bore witness first-hand to General Brock's historic journey to meet with Chief Tecumseh on August 13, 1812. This meeting led to the capture of Fort Detroit and British control of the Michigan frontier; more than 2,000 muskets were captured and used to arm Canadian militia units. In the later 1800s, Loyalists from the area fought in the Fenian raids; many served in World Wars I and II in an effort to preserve our history, our land, and our stake in the future.

Kingsville's harbour provides shelter for ships in need and provides commerce for the area.

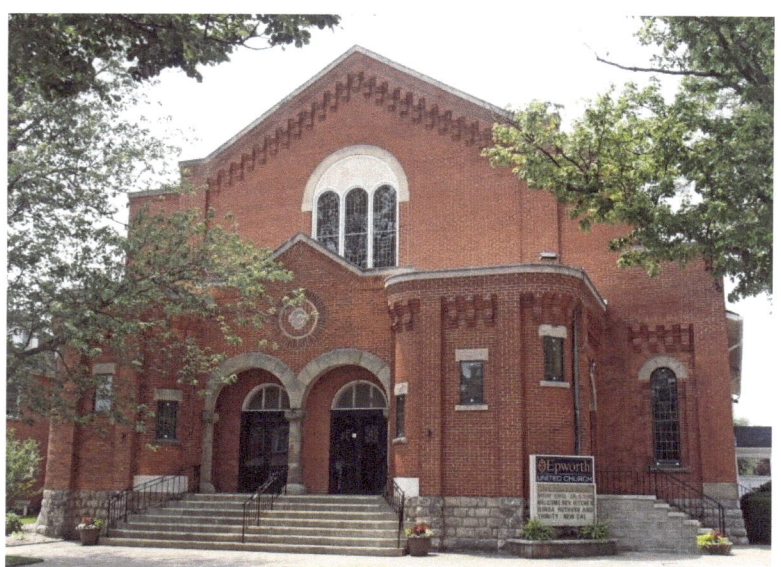

56 Division Street South - Epworth United Church - 1893
Bevelled dentil moulding

In 1817 a small log Methodist chapel was built in the Kingsville area. Property for the church at its current location was purchased in 1891 and construction completed in 1893. In honor of John Wesley, the founder of Methodism, the new church was called Epworth Methodist Church, after his birthplace of Epworth Rectory in England. After the union of the Methodists, Presbyterians and Congregationalists in 1925, the name became Epworth United Church. A devastating fire in 1935 destroyed a large portion of the old church. The current structure is the result of a rebuilding effort that began the same year and completed in 1936.

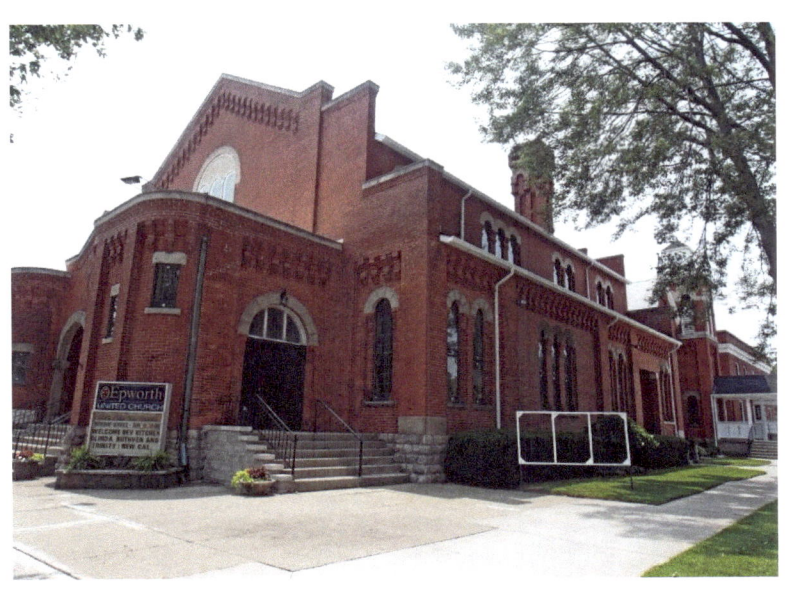

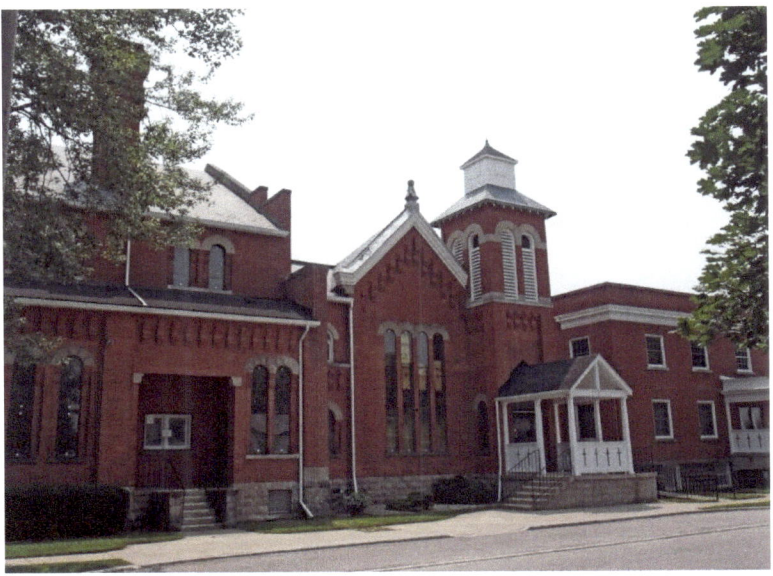

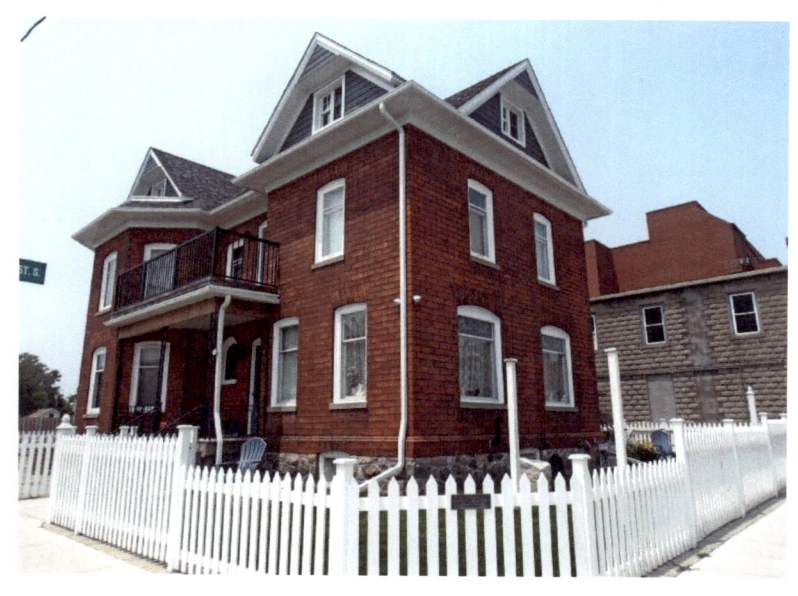

Division Street North – Edwardian style

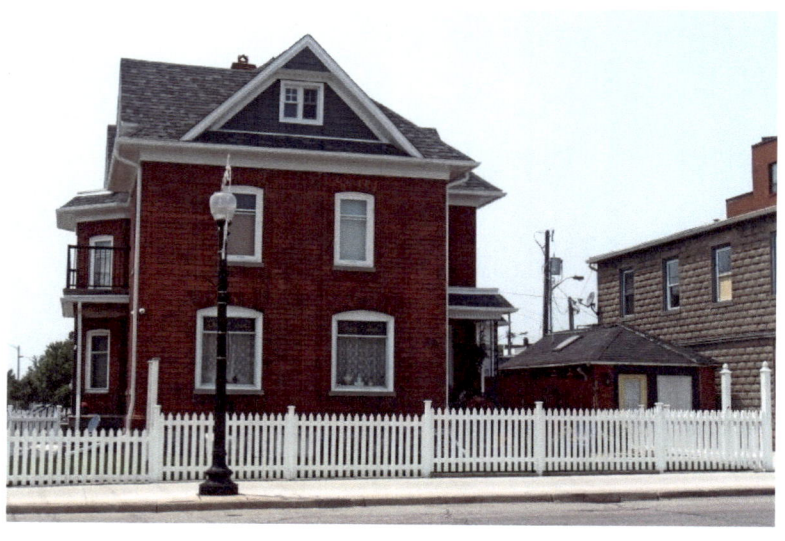

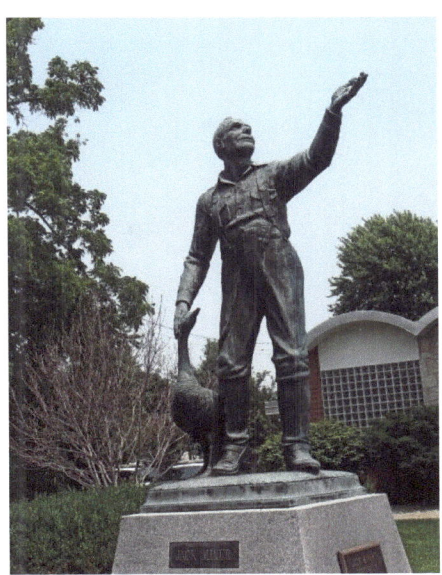

Jack Minor's Testimony

The Lord is my guide and teacher, I will not get lost;
He makes my heart a receiving station for his wireless;
He sits down beside me in the pathless woods and opens up
his book of knowledge;
He turns the leaves very slowly that my dimmed eyes may
read his meaning;
He makes the trees I plant to grow, and flowers to arch my
path with their fragrant beauty,
Gives me dominion over the fowls of the air and they honk
and sing their way to and from my home.
Yea, he has brought me up from a barefooted
underpriviledged boy to a man respected by millions of
people, and I give him all the credit and praise whenever,
wherever, and forever.

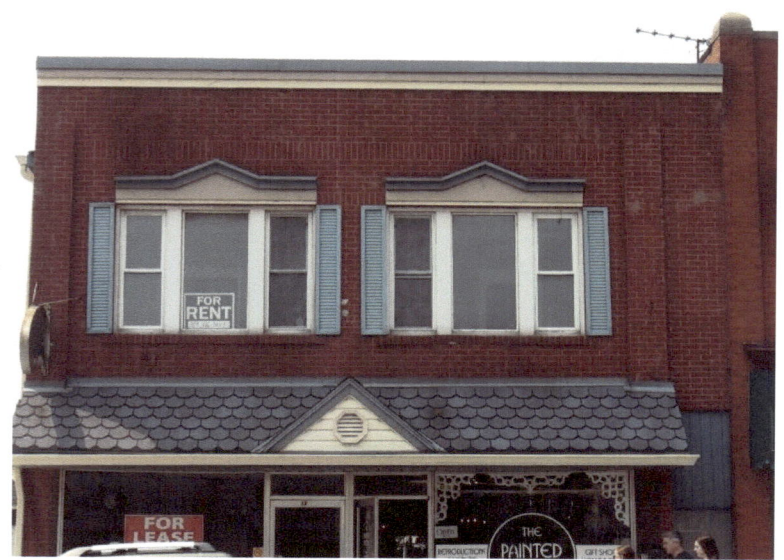

18 Division Street – pilasters and decorative window hoods

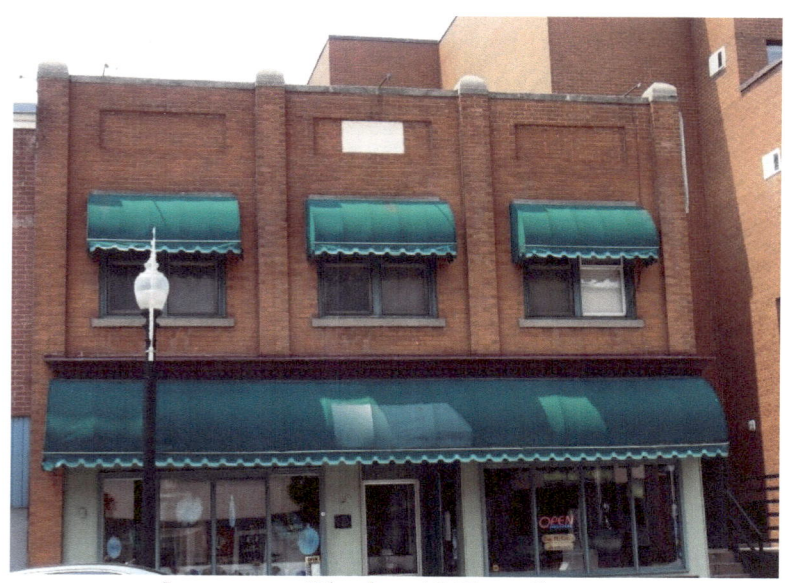

Jasperson Block – 1915 - pilasters

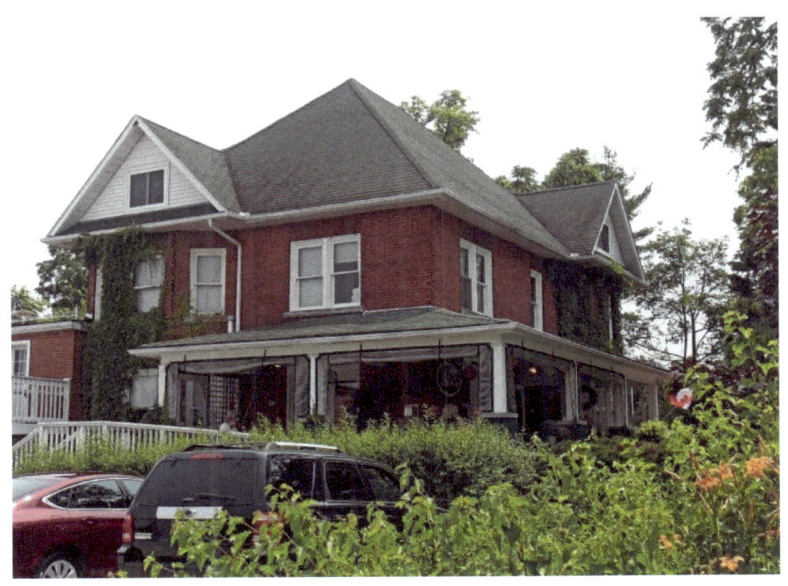

31 Division Street South – Jack's Gastropub and Inn
Colonial Revival style

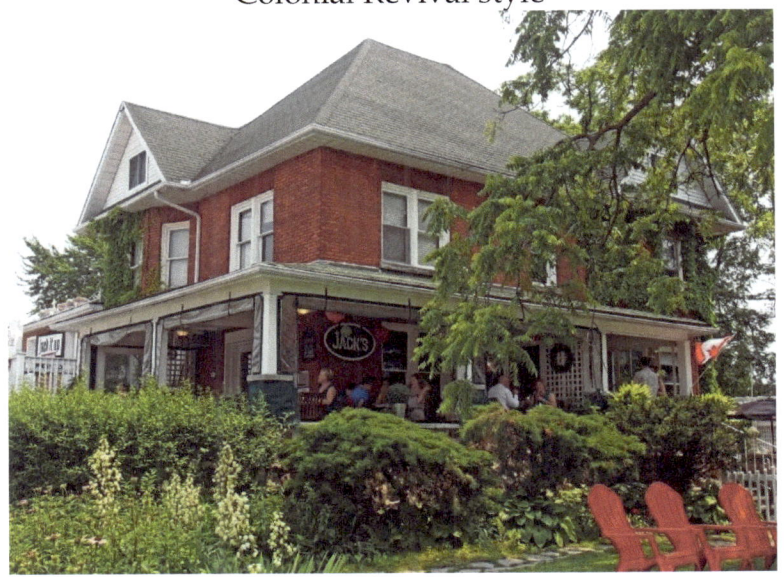

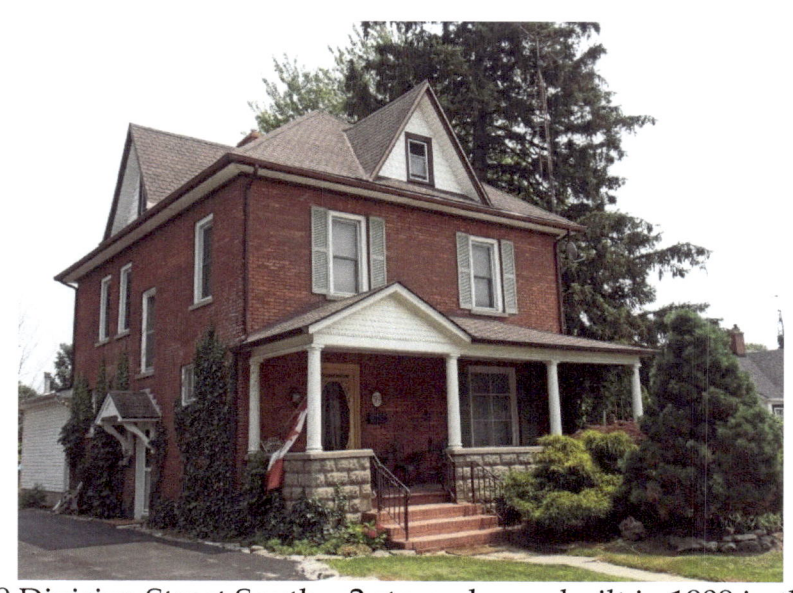

59 Division Street South – 2 storey house built in 1909 in the Colonial Revival style – cut fieldstone foundation, hip roof, doric columns,

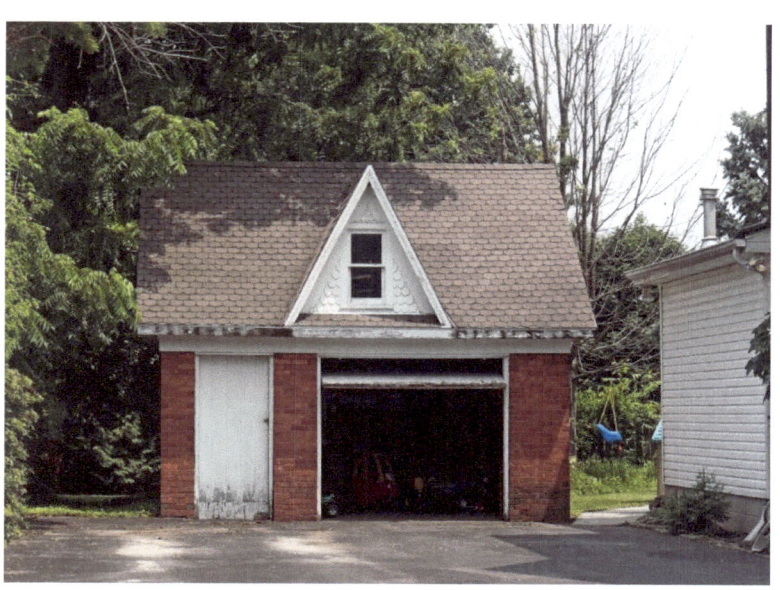

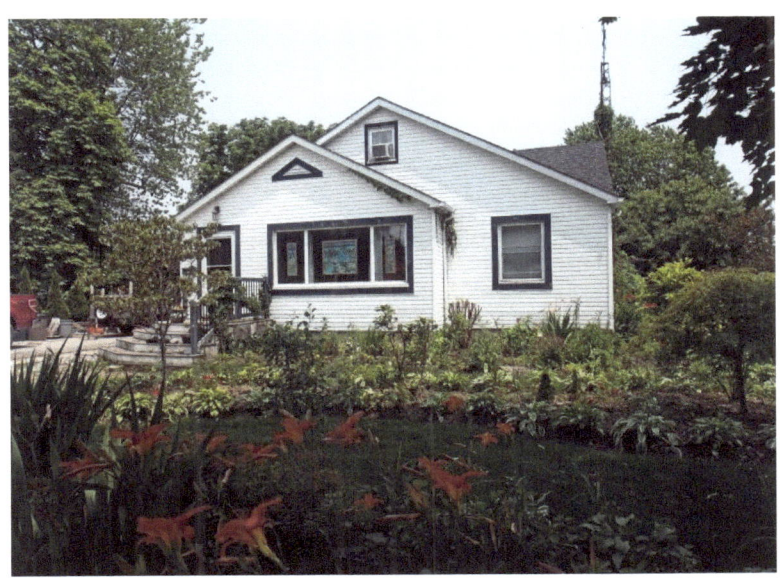

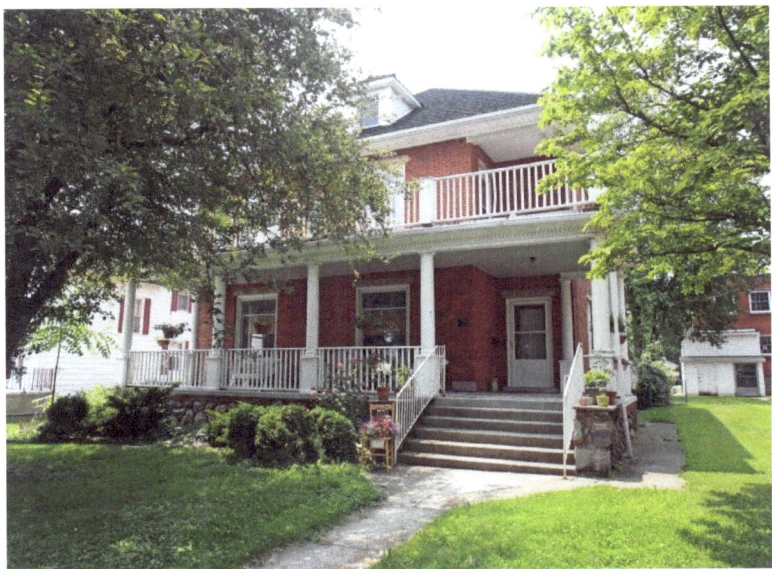

62 Division Street South - Epworth Parsonage built 1908 – Colonial Revival style, hip roof, dormers, doric columns and full width two-storey wraparound porch

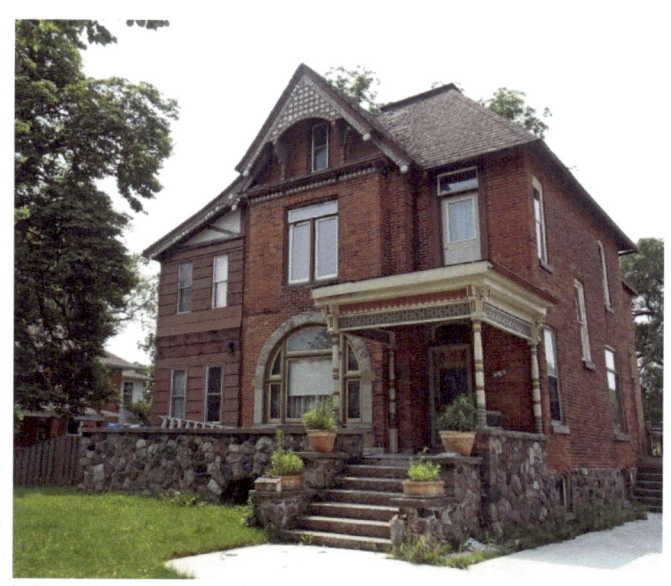

78 Division Street South– built in 1893 in Queen Anne style, front gable with basket weave cross-bracing with decorative verge boards, fretwork, 2½ storey rectangular bay with herringbone brick pattern to separate second storey from attic, cut fieldstone foundation, transom windows, large first storey arched window with rough and smooth stone surround

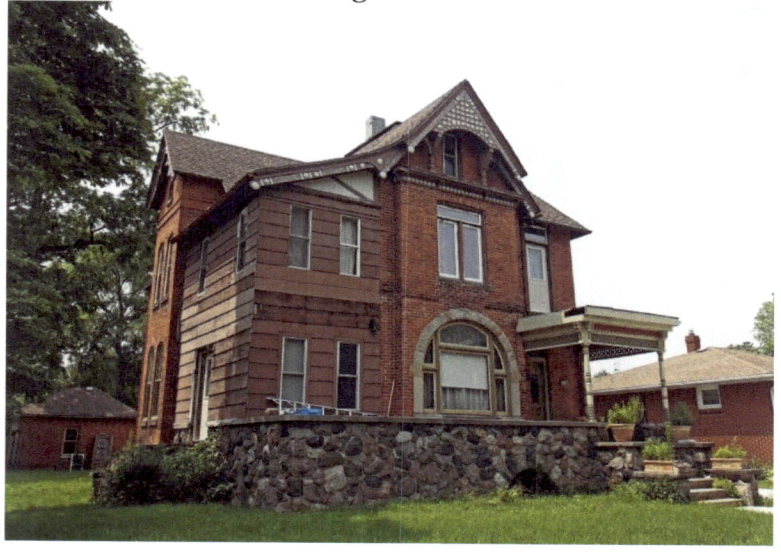

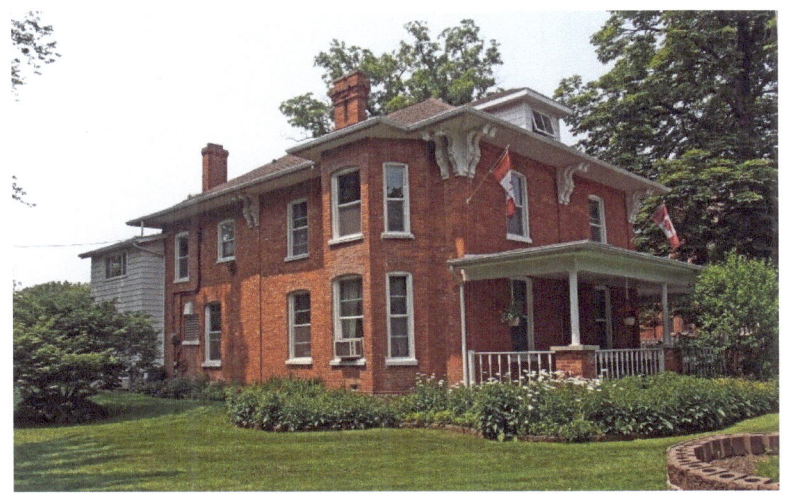

86 Division Street South – 2-storey brick house built in 1882 in the Italianate style, hipped roof, paired cornice brackets, dormer, cut fieldstone foundation, three large brick chimneys

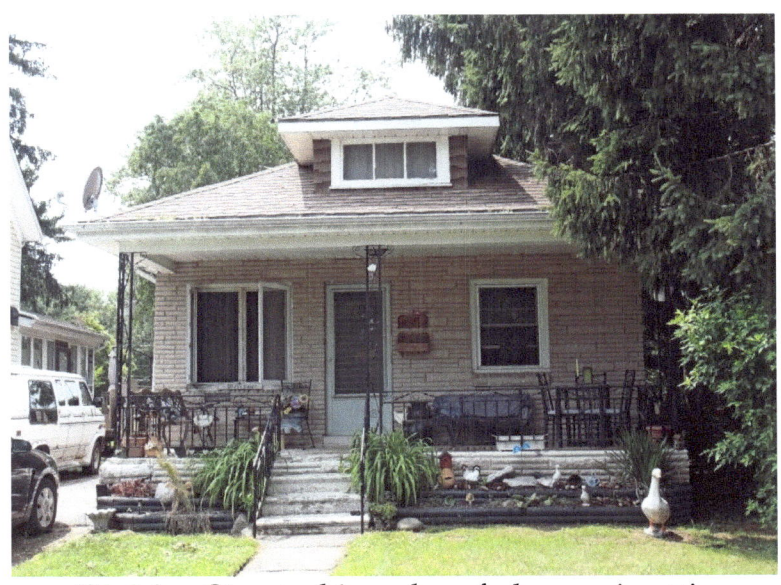

Division Street – hipped roof, dormer in attic

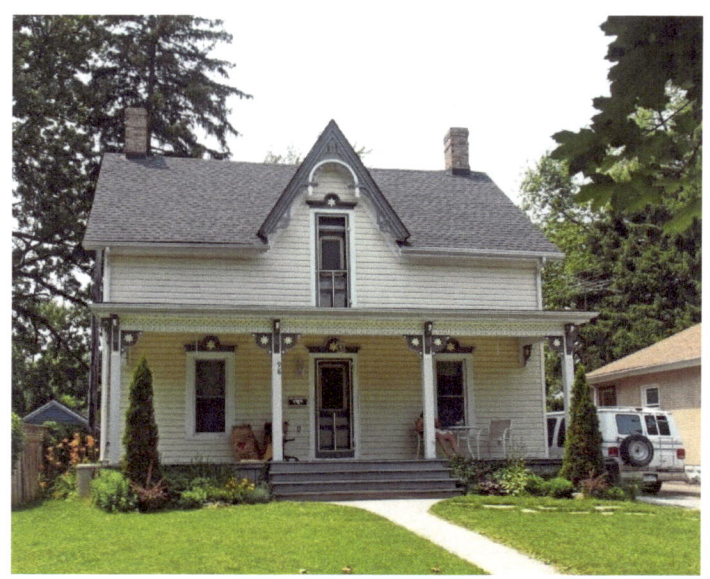

98 Division Street – Gothic Revival style, verge board trim on gable, decorative window hood above second floor door, decorative woodwork on verandah cornice and pillars

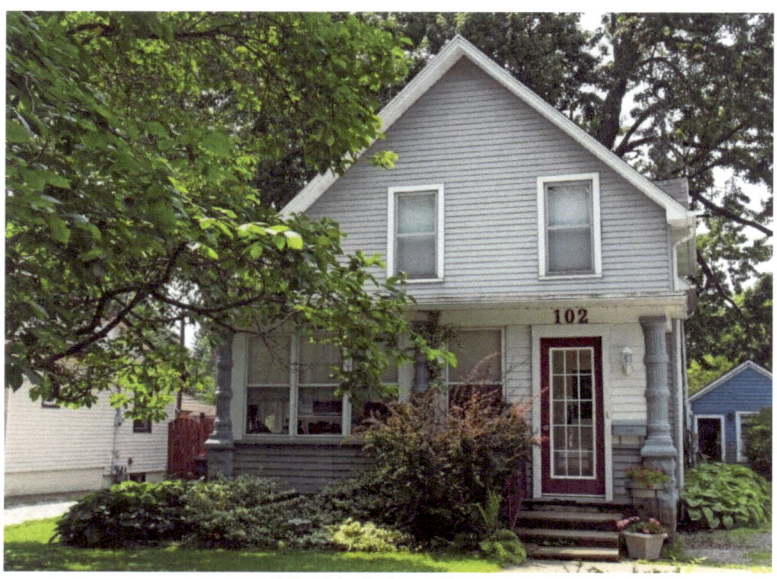

102 Division Street

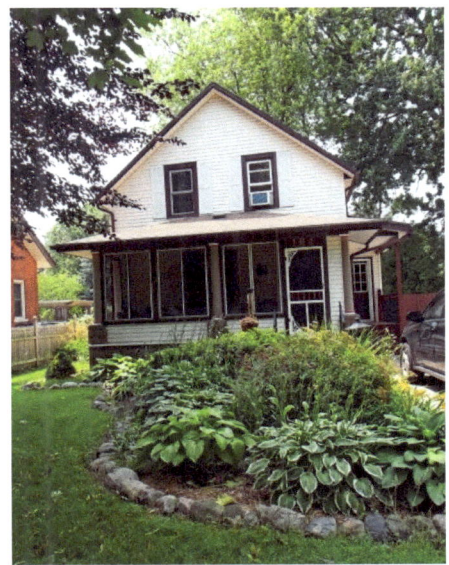

104 Division Street

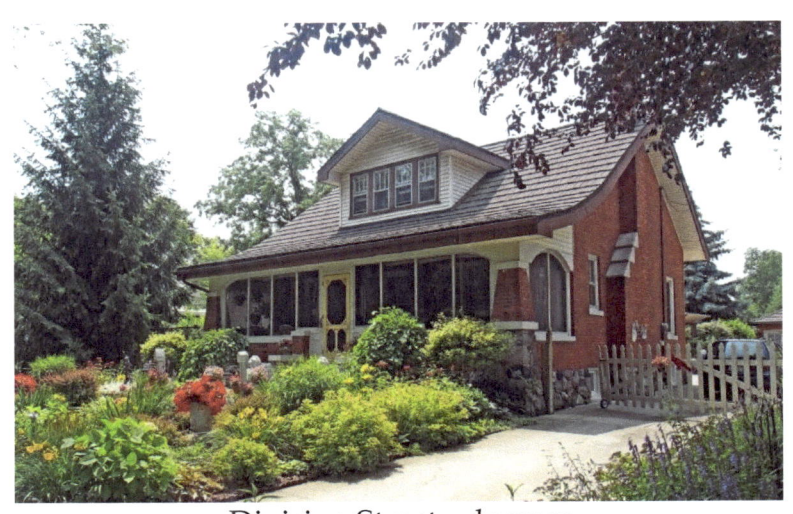

Division Street - dormer

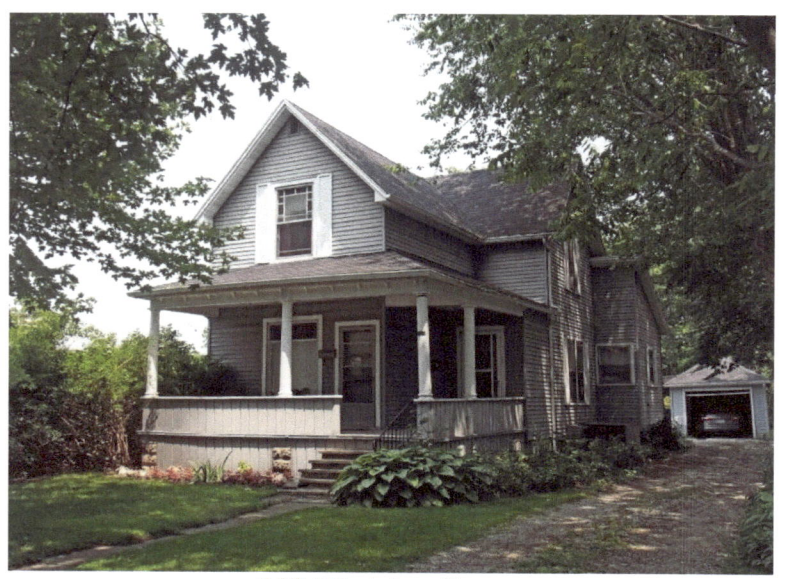

103 Division Street

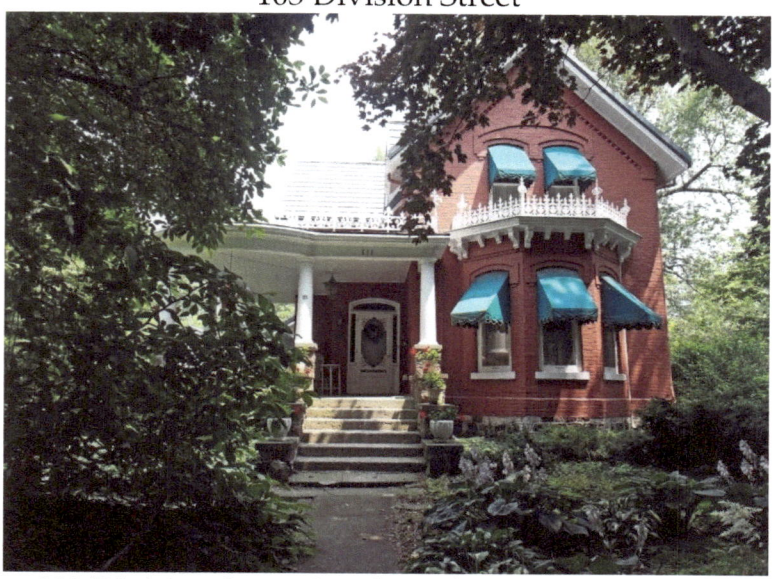

111 Division Street South – 1½ storey Gothic Villa
Cut fieldstone foundation, large curved verandah, wide brick
trim in gable, iron cresting above bay window with
cornice brackets

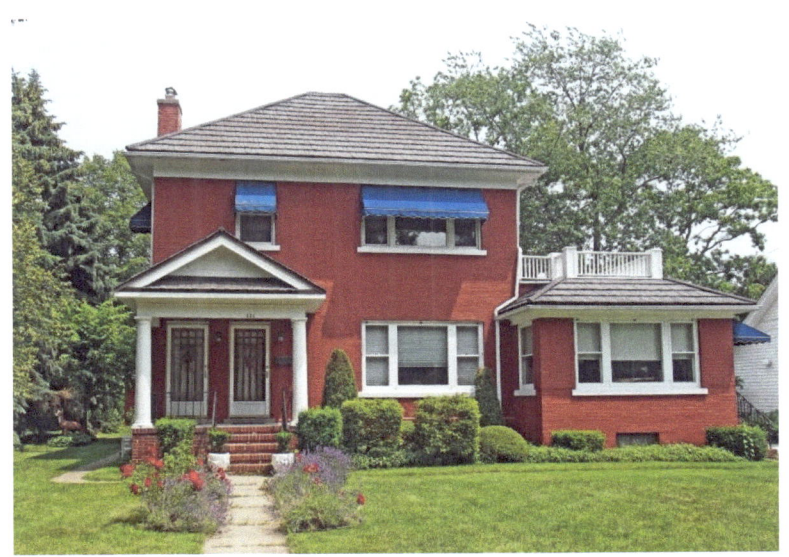

121 Division Street – pediment above double front doors, doric pillars, second floor balcony

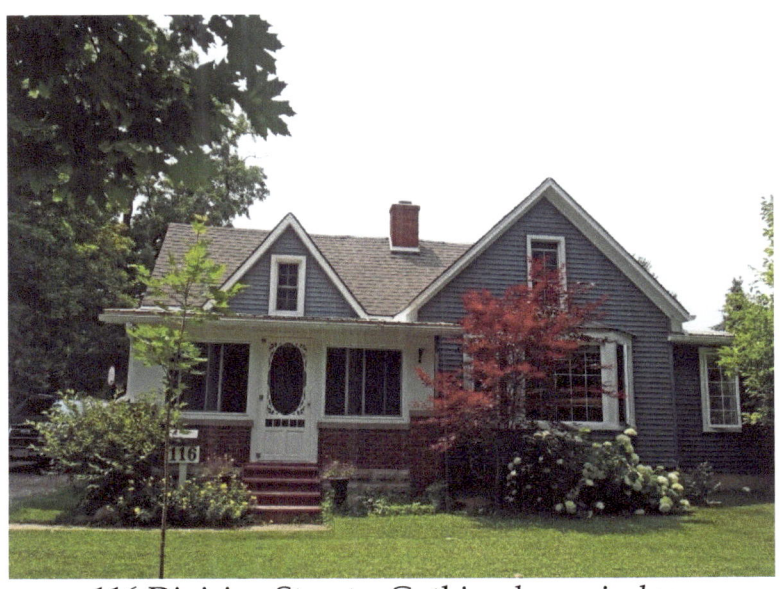

116 Division Street – Gothic – bay window

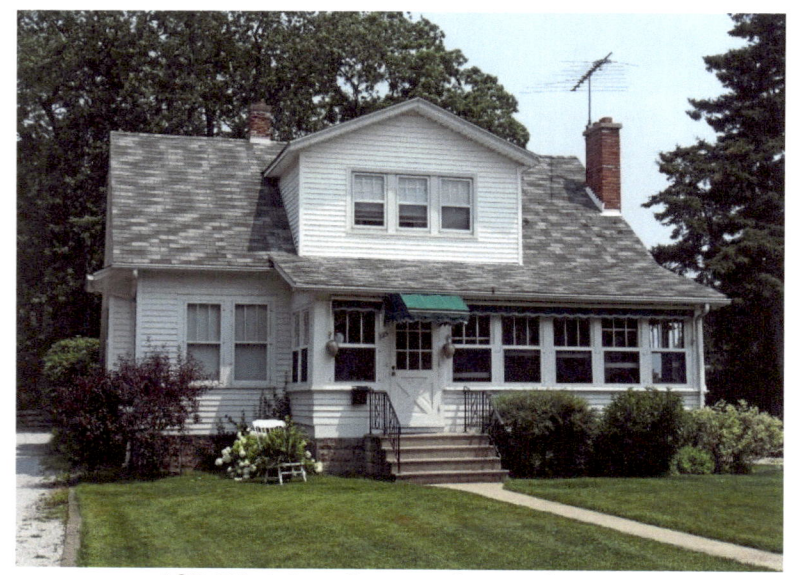

125 Division Street – large dormer

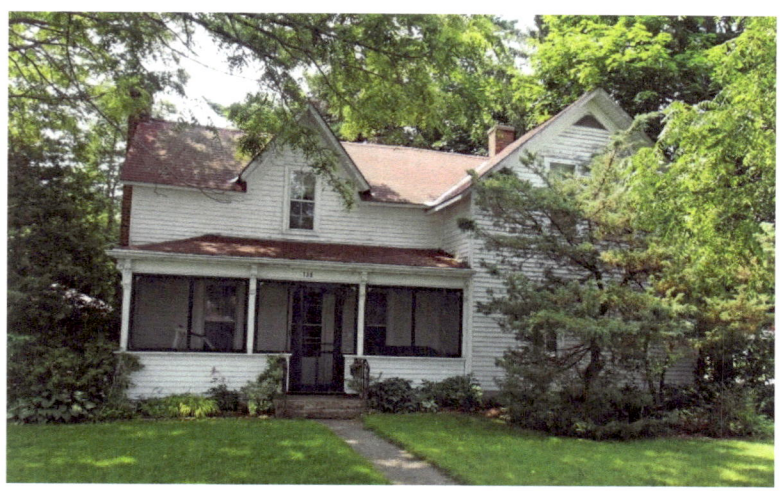

138 Division Street - Gothic

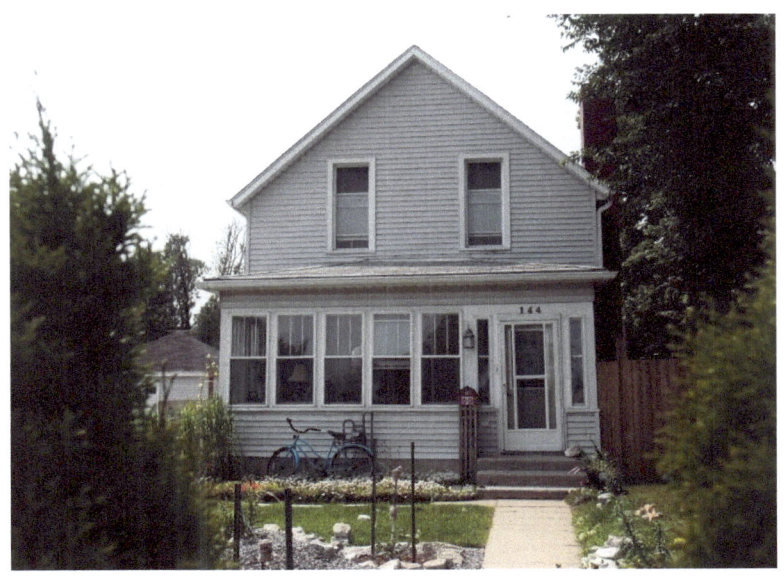

144 Division Street

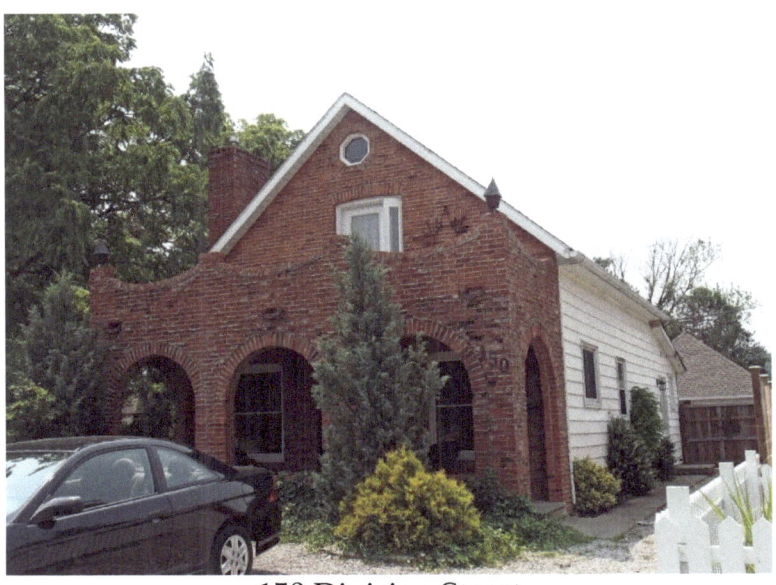

150 Division Street

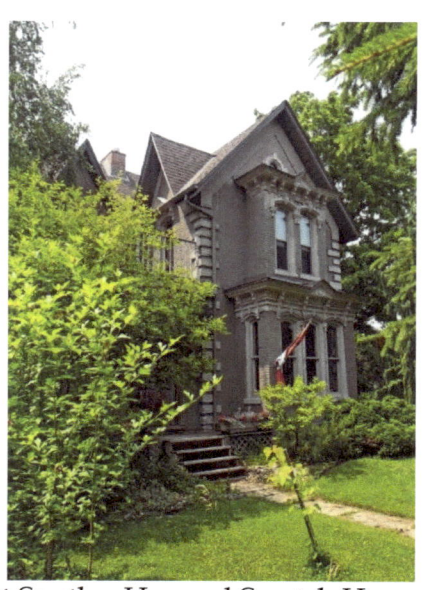

164 Division Street South – Howard Scratch House – 2 storey – 1886 – Italianate style (Scratch was a local tinsmith and bicycle factory owner) – asymmetrical design; brick quoins on corners; roundel windows in each of three large gables; 2-storey square bay on the front of the house; 1-storey angular bay on the north side; one-over-one double hung wood sash windows

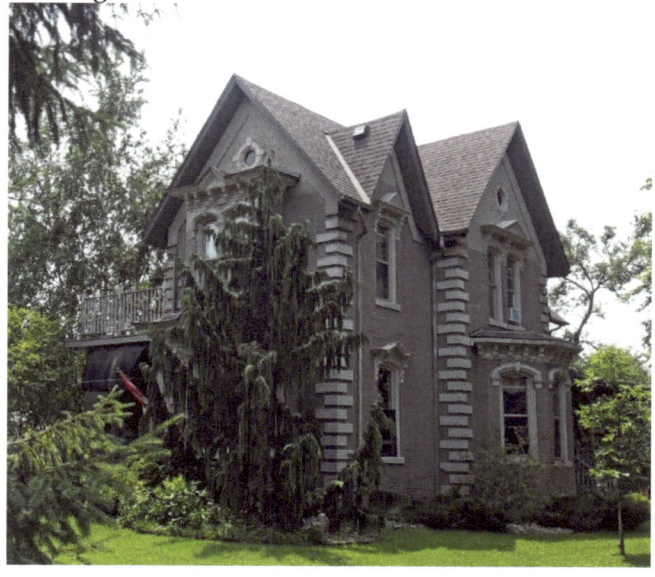

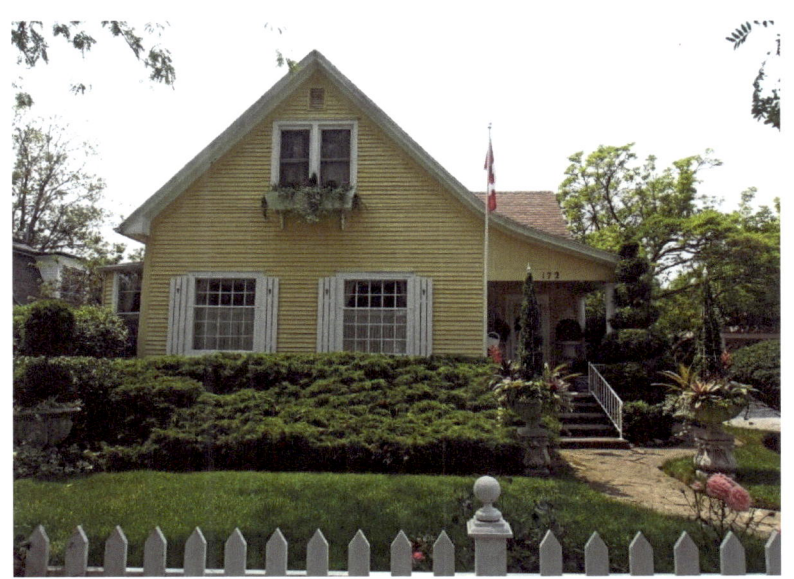

172 Division Street

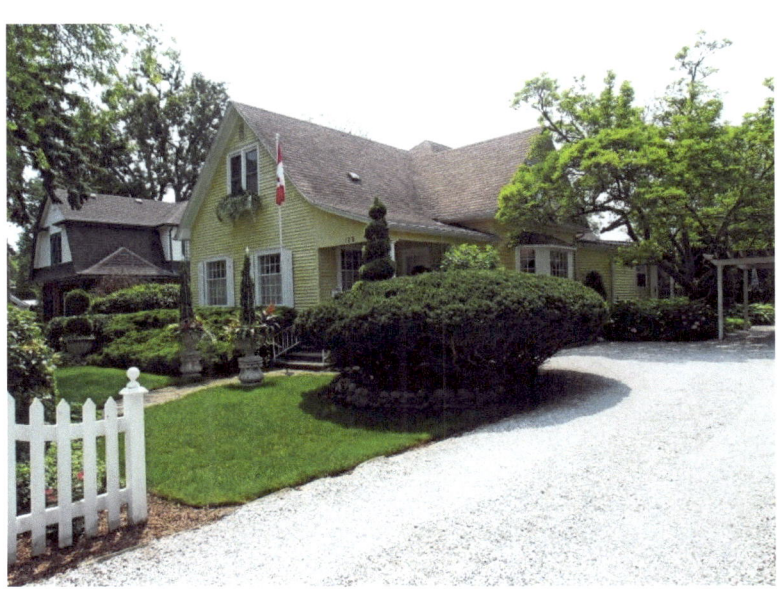

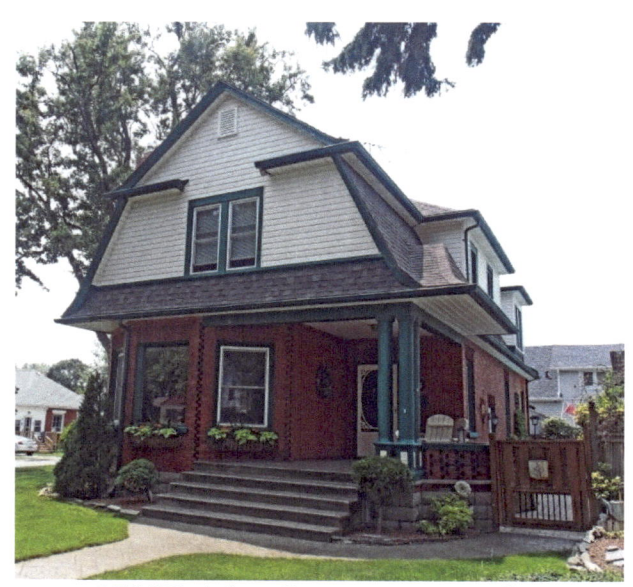

176 Division Street – vernacular

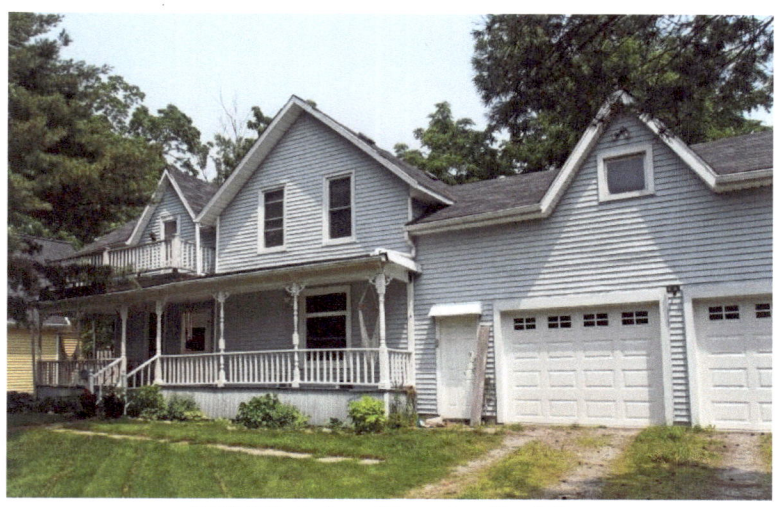

162 Division Street - Gothic

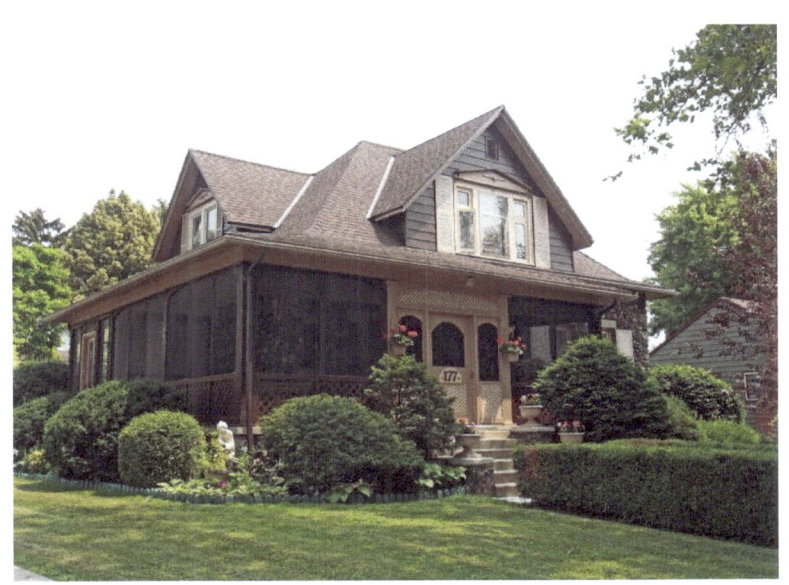

177 Division Street

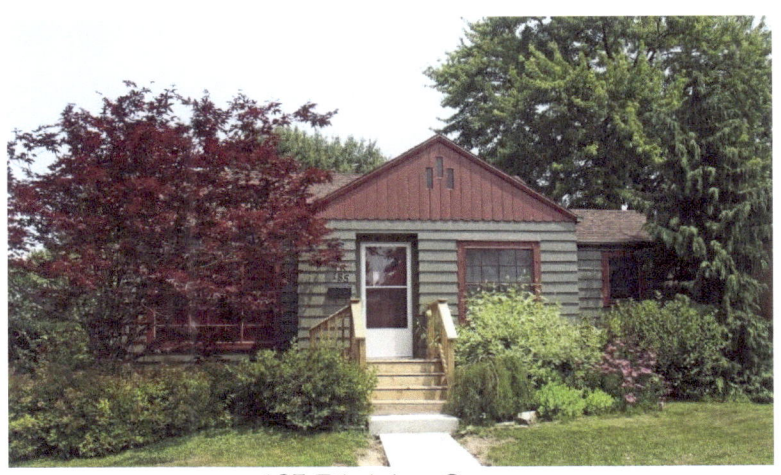

185 Division Street

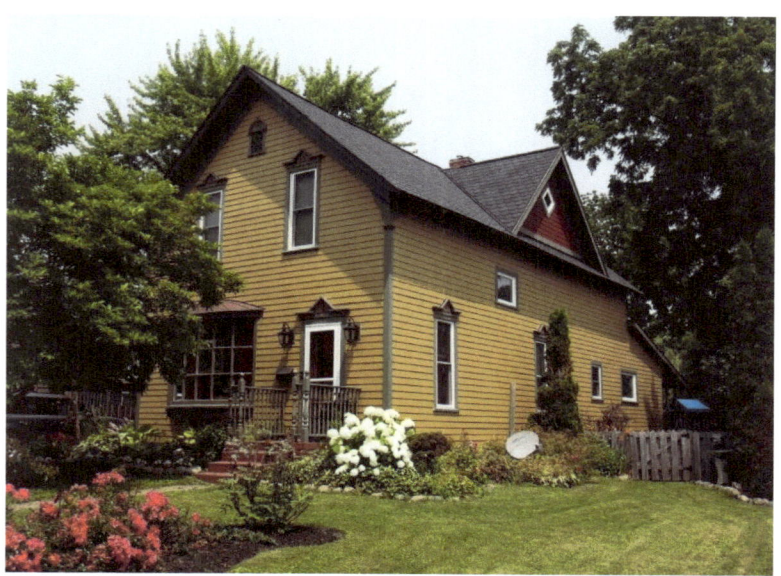

189 Division Street – John Malott House – 1½ storey – 1887 –
Folk Victorian style – triangular pediments inset with applied
scrollwork above the windows and front door; wood exterior
doors with arched windows

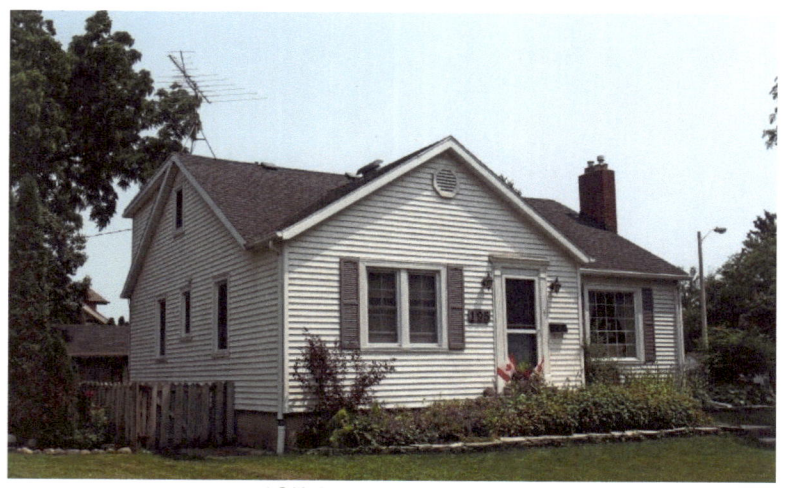

195 Division Street

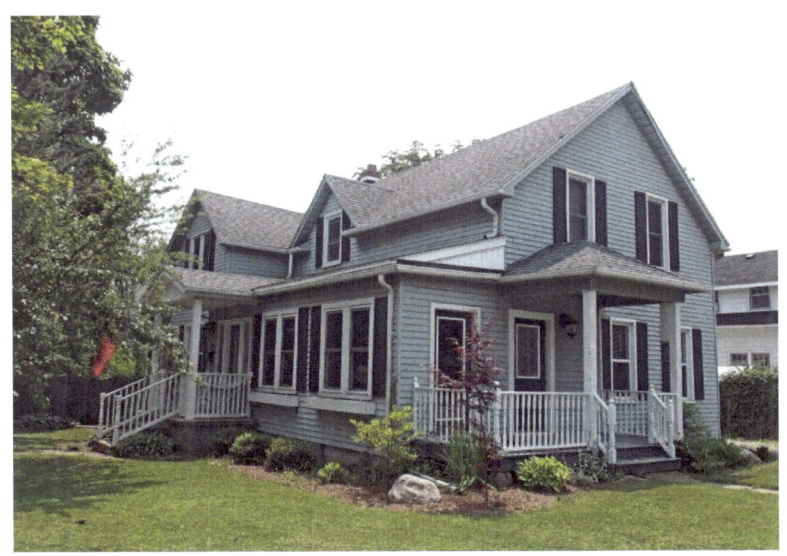

Division Street – Gothic

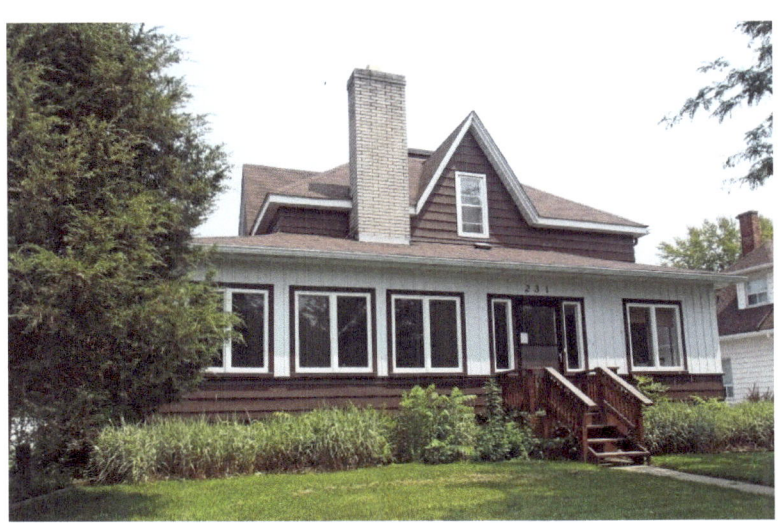

231 Division Street - Gothic

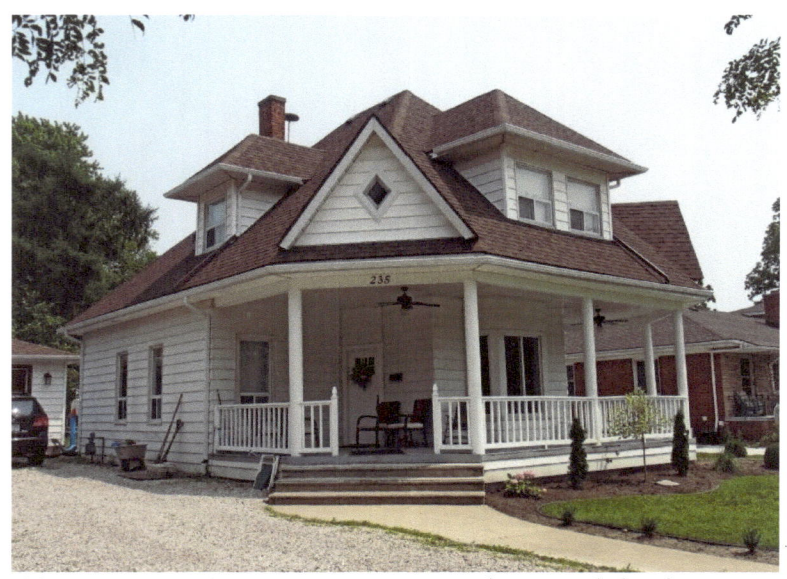

235 Division Street – wraparound verandah, dormers

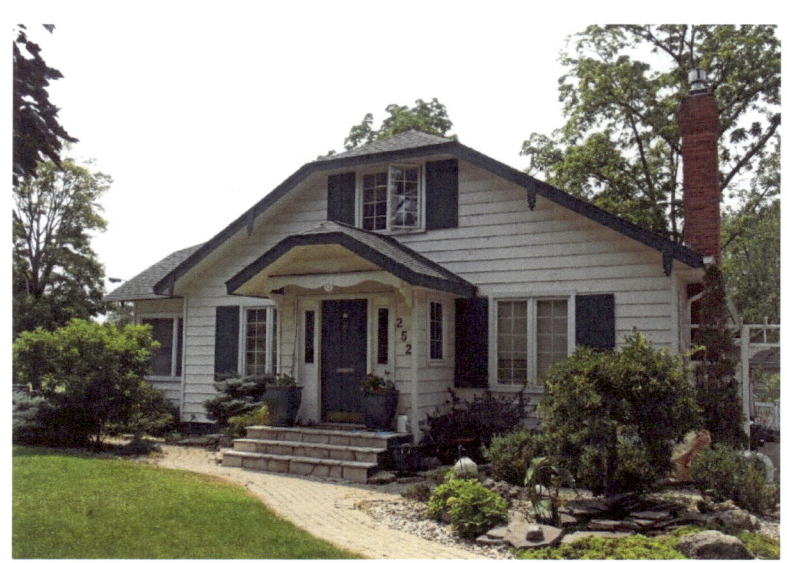

252 Division Street

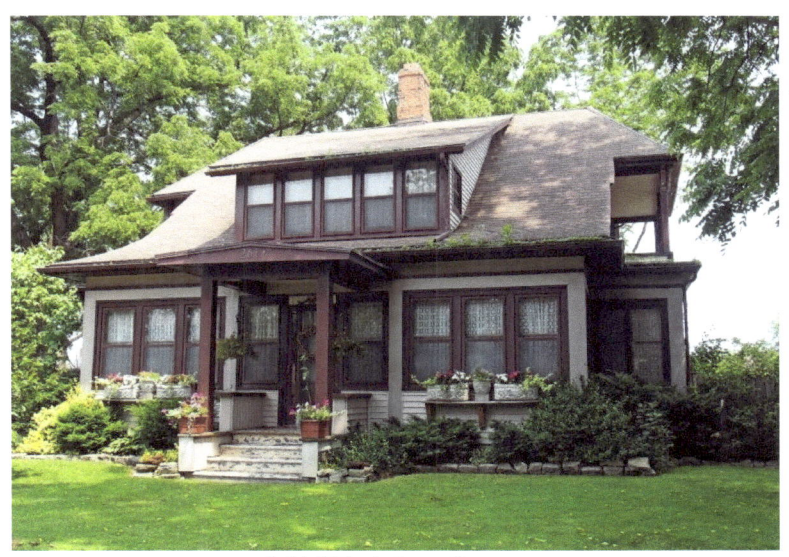

261 Division Street

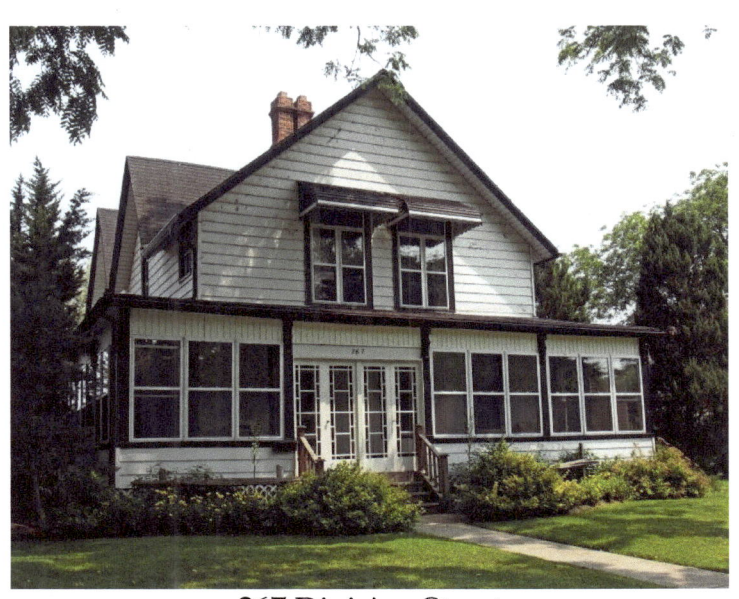

267 Division Street

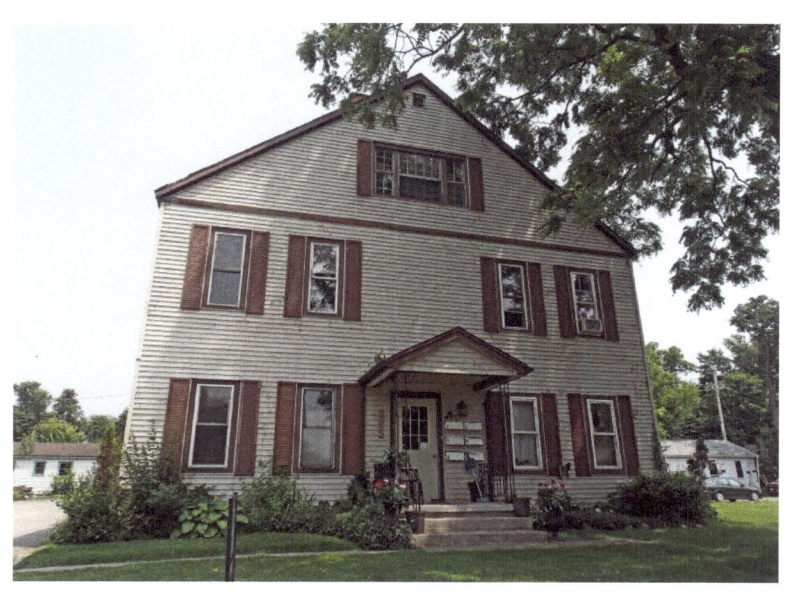

285 Division Street - Georgian

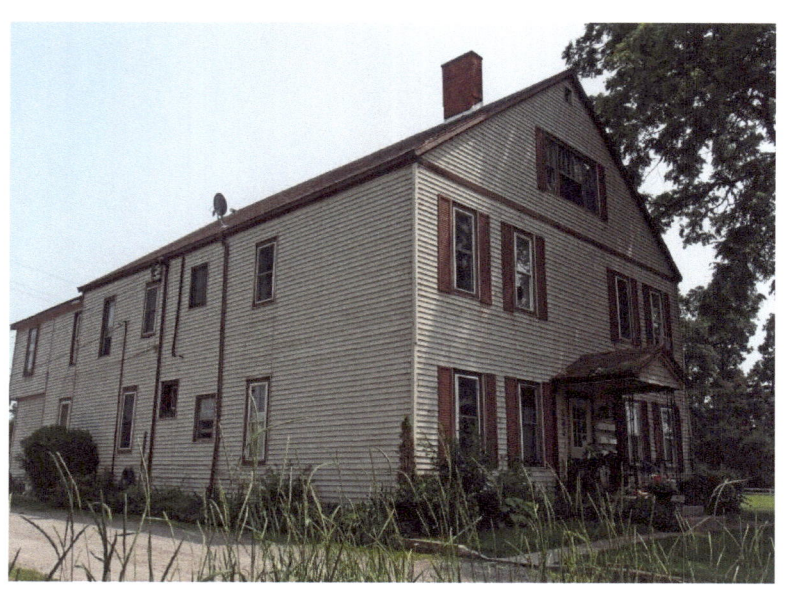

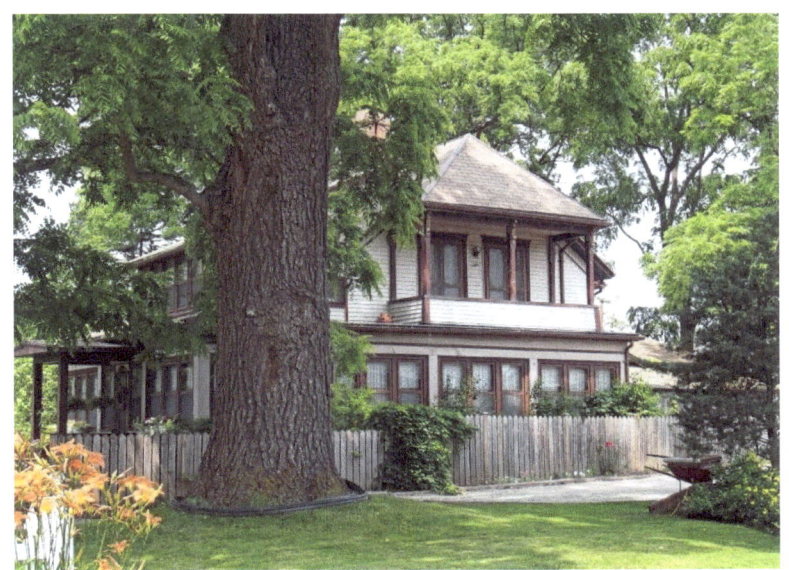

Division Street

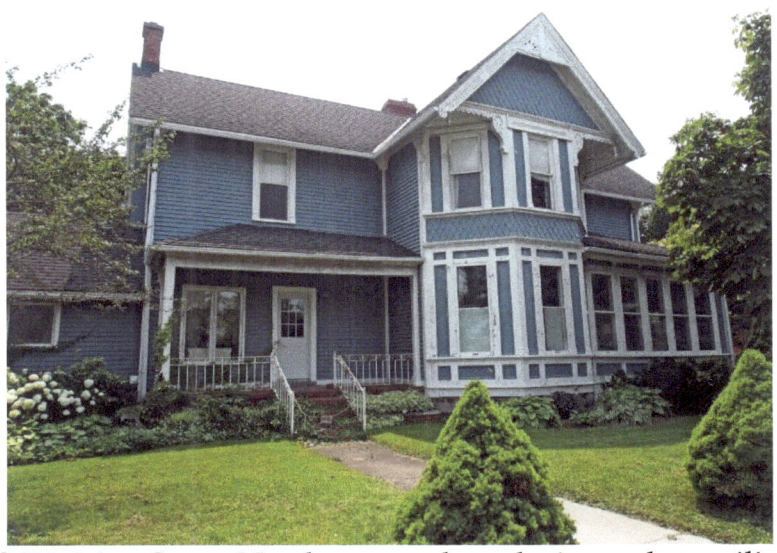

53 Division Street North – verge board trim and stenciling

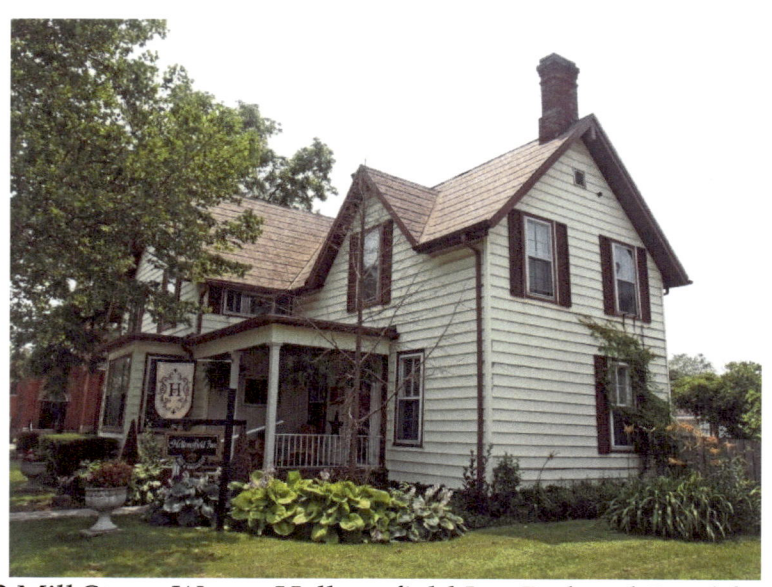

2 Mill Street West – Hellemsfield Inn Bed and Breakfast
Gothic Revival style built in 1872 – 1½ storey, field stone
foundation – original cladding is oak board and batten now
covered with aluminum siding

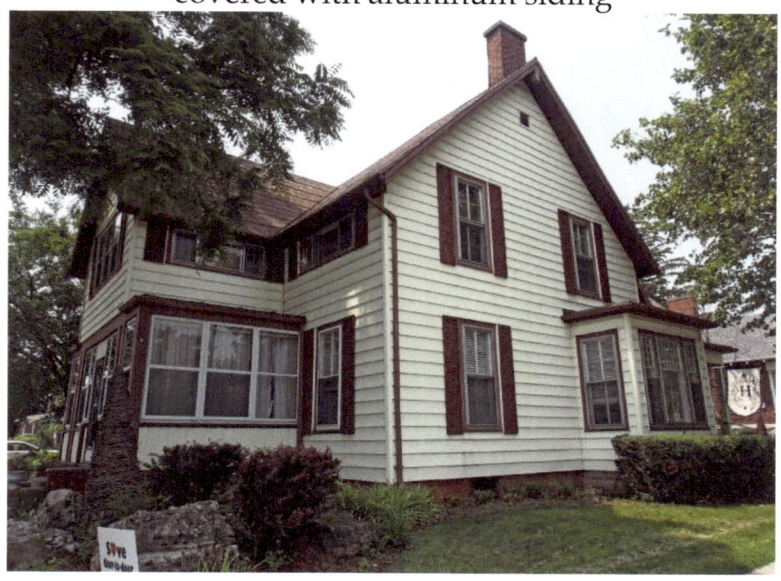

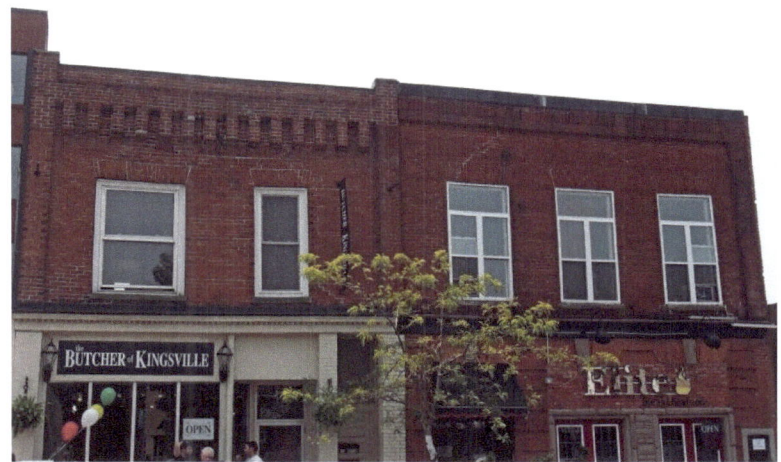

Main Street West – pilasters, bevelled dentil moulding

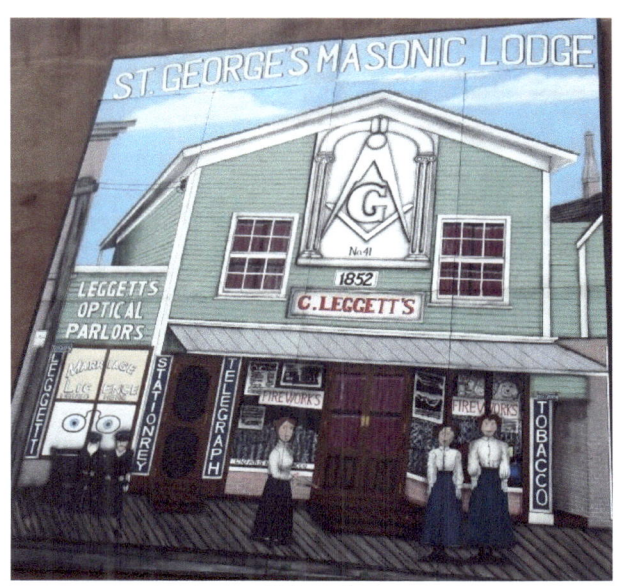

Mural

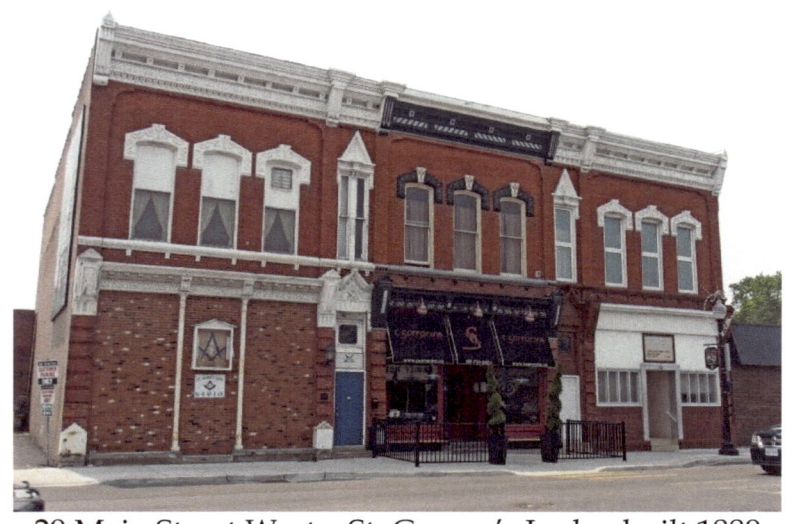

29 Main Street West – St. George's Lodge built 1889
2-storey Italianate style; bracketed cornices and dentils;
segmental arches and pilasters; decorative window hoods;
belt course projects beyond the face of the building

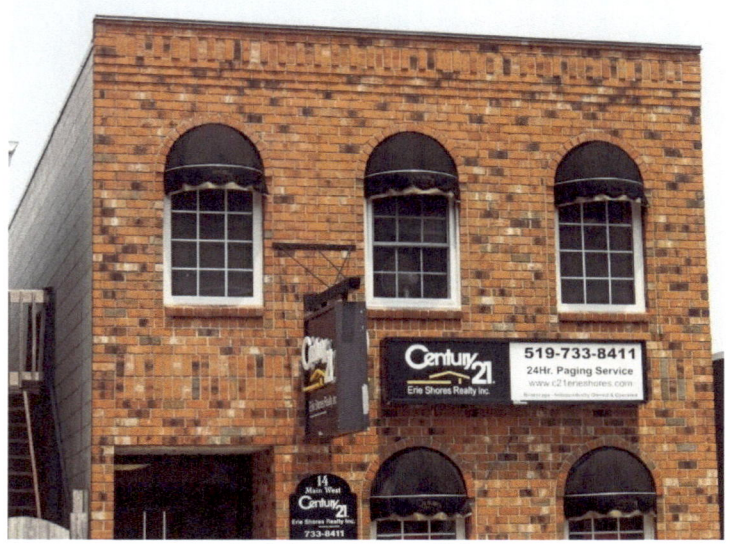

14 Main Street West

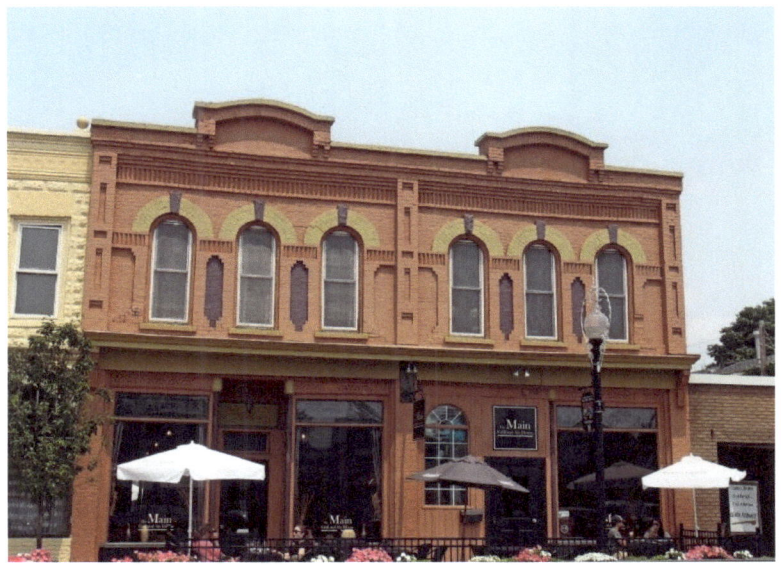

Main Street West – pilasters, dentil moulding, window voussoirs and keystones

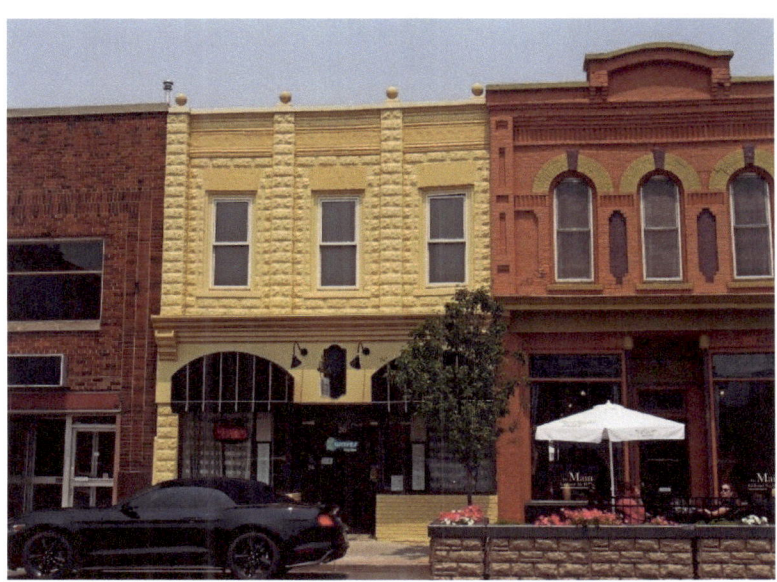

26 Main Street West – pilasters, decorative brickwork

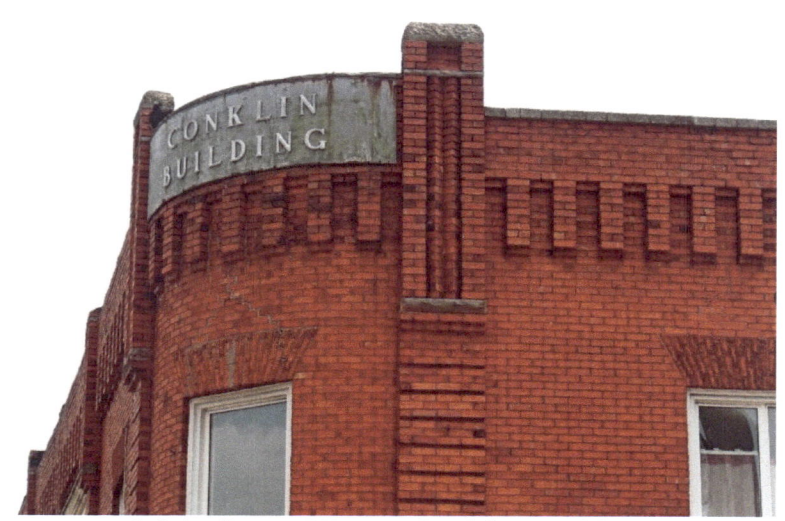

Main Street West – Conklin Building

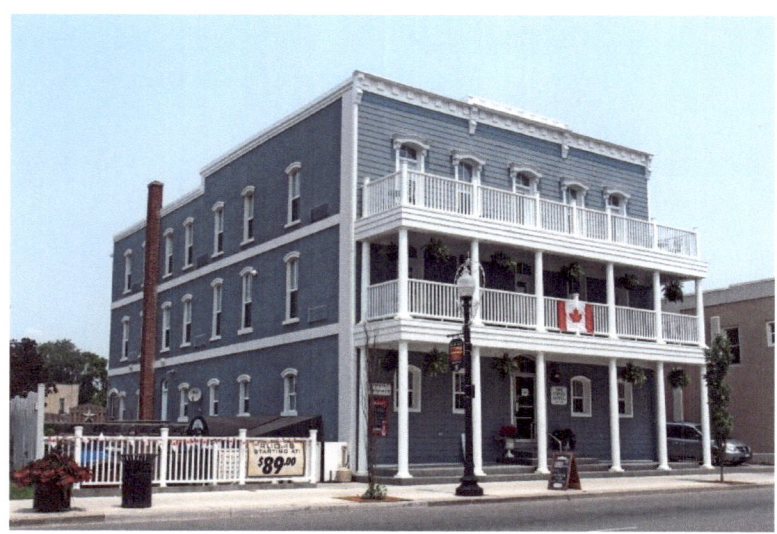

12 Main Street East – The King's Hotel established 1885 with 3rd storey added in 1889 – window hoods on 3rd floor

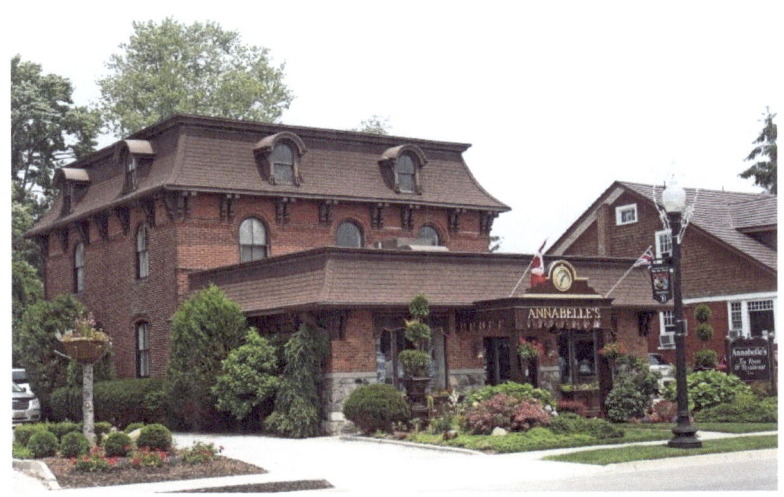

76 Main Street East – Annabelle's Tea House and Restaurant
Built in 1859 – Second Empire style – dormers with window
hoods in mansard roof, paired cornice brackets

Anna Belle Miriah Brien Evans was Susanne's grandmother, for whom tea was an essential part of her day. Tea time for her grandma was an institution. At 4 o'clock, as matter-of-factly as anything done on a regular basis, she would proceed to the kitchen as if reminded by an internal clock. Susanne would get the small china tea set and set the table by the window in the dining room. There, as the sunlight streamed in, they would sip tea, have a biscuit, or two, and talk about the day.

These are childhood memories that Susanne cherishes. In her honour, she created a place for people to spend time together and perhaps create lovely memories of their own. Tea time has a way of making an ordinary day an occasion.

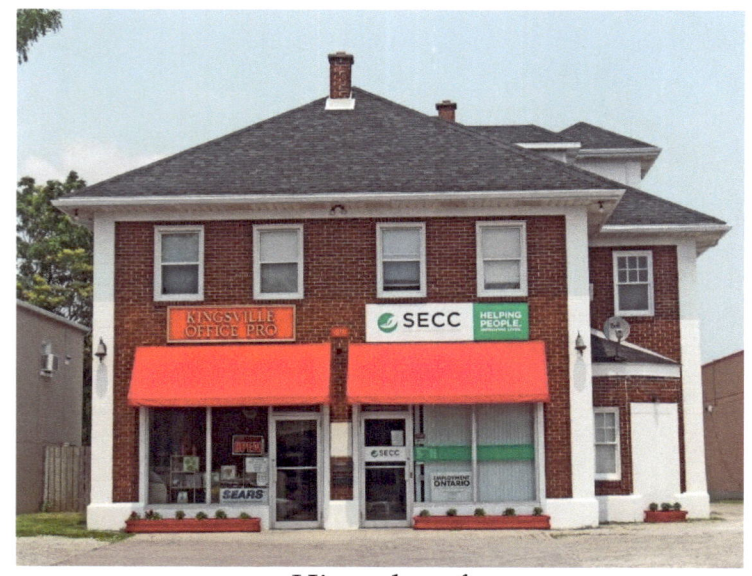

Hipped roof

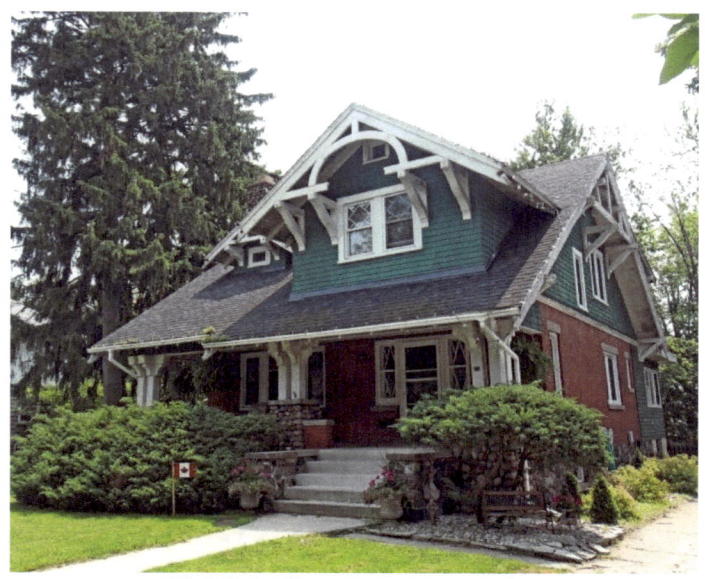

93 Main Street - vernacular

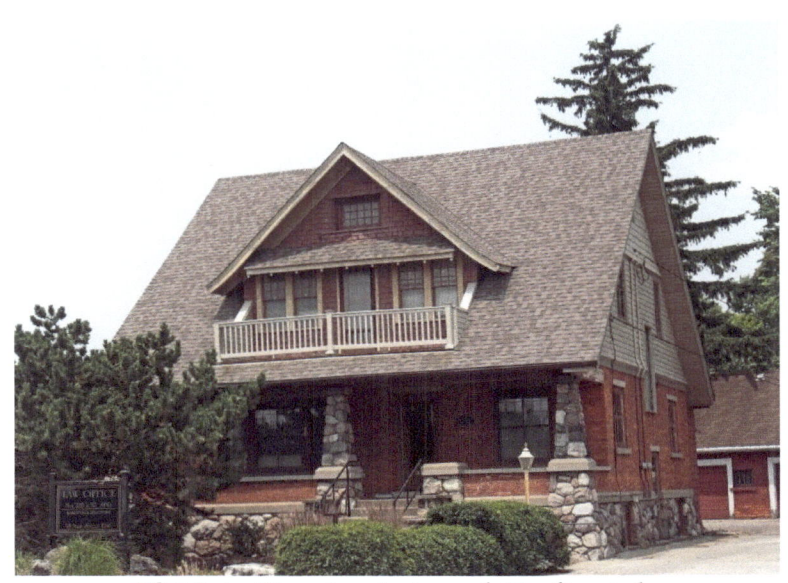

58 Main Street – Arts and Crafts style

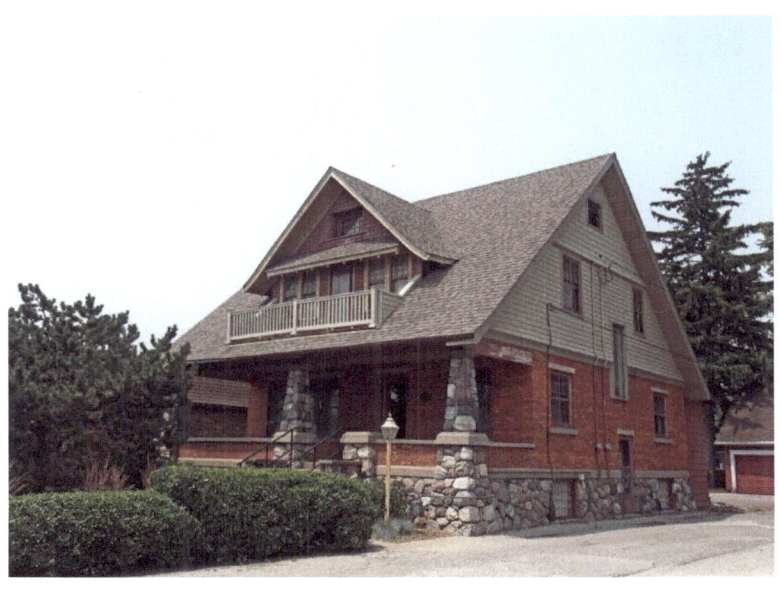

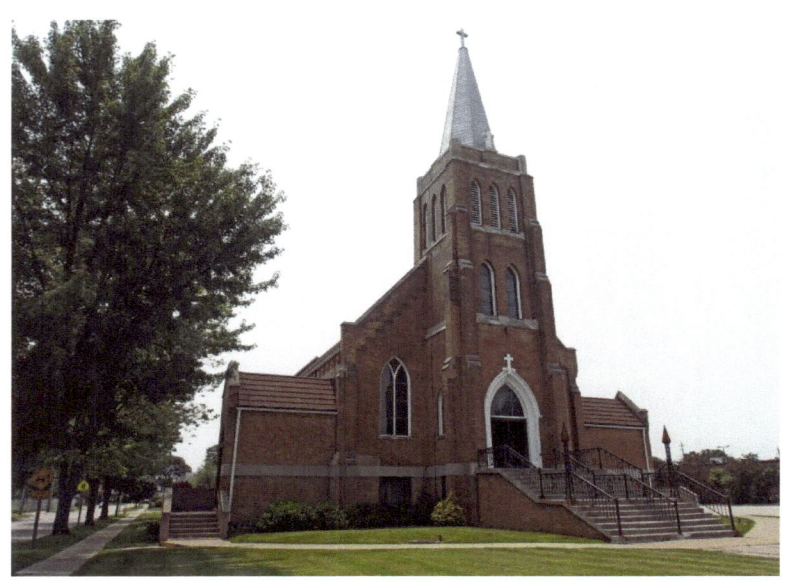

67 Main Street East – St. John de Brebeuf Roman Catholic
Church – buttresses, lancet windows, dentil moulding

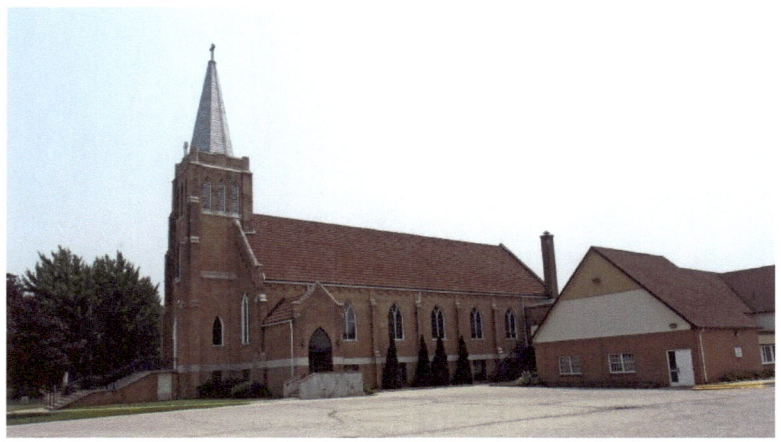

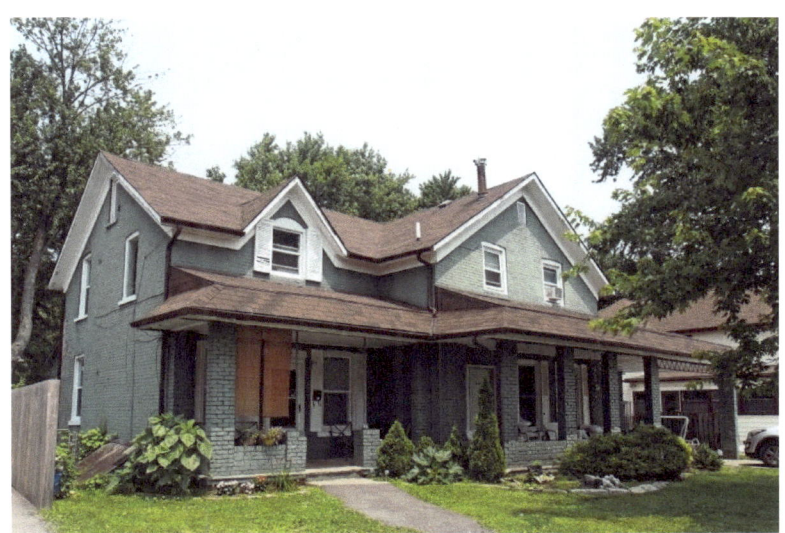

104 Main Street East – Gothic Revival

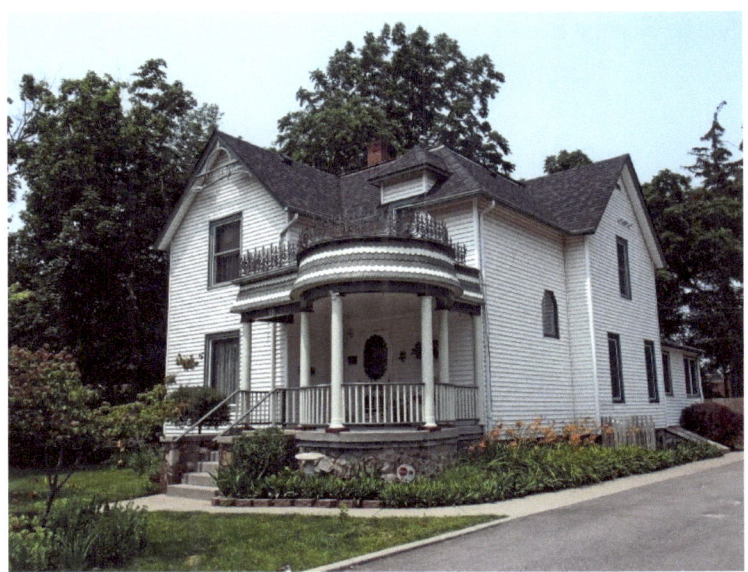

98 Main Street East – built 1905 – Queen Anne Revival style
The "Wedding Cake House" – fish-scale trim around top of porch
resembles icing on a wedding cake – gingerbread wood scroll work
in gables, iron cresting around second floor balcony above semi-
circular porch

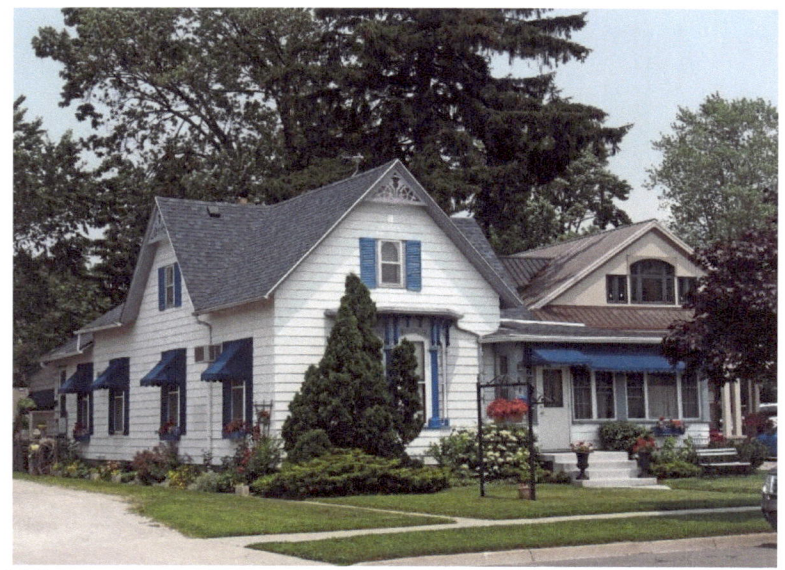

64 Main Street East – Gothic – verge board trim on gable

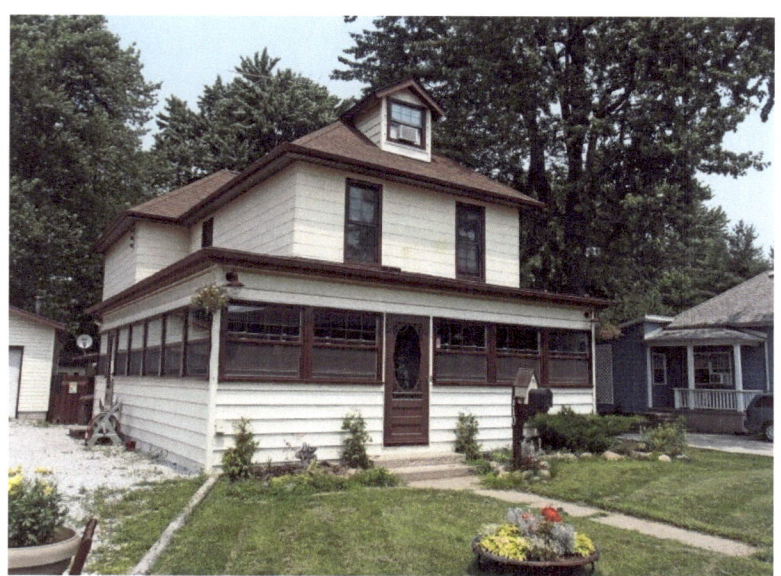

110 Main Street East

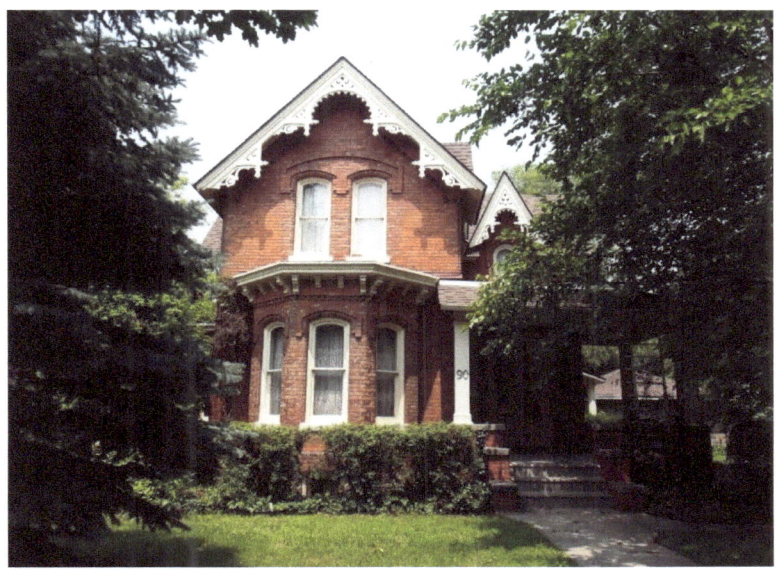

90 Main Street East – The Jacob Wigle/William Mortan Webb House built 1886 – Gothic Revival – verge board trim on gable, bay window, decorative brickwork including sawtooth designs, hood moulds over the windows

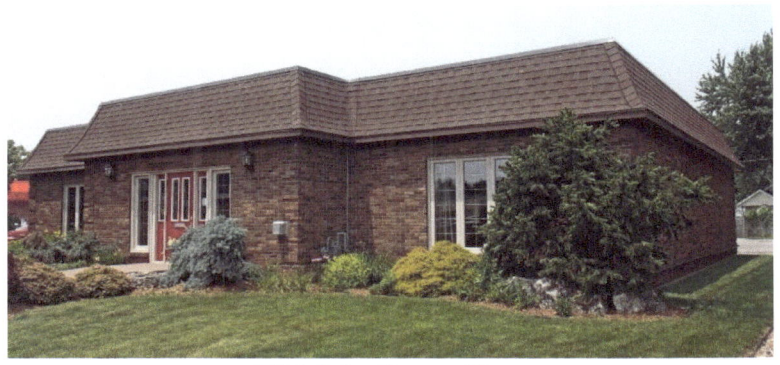

50 Main Street East

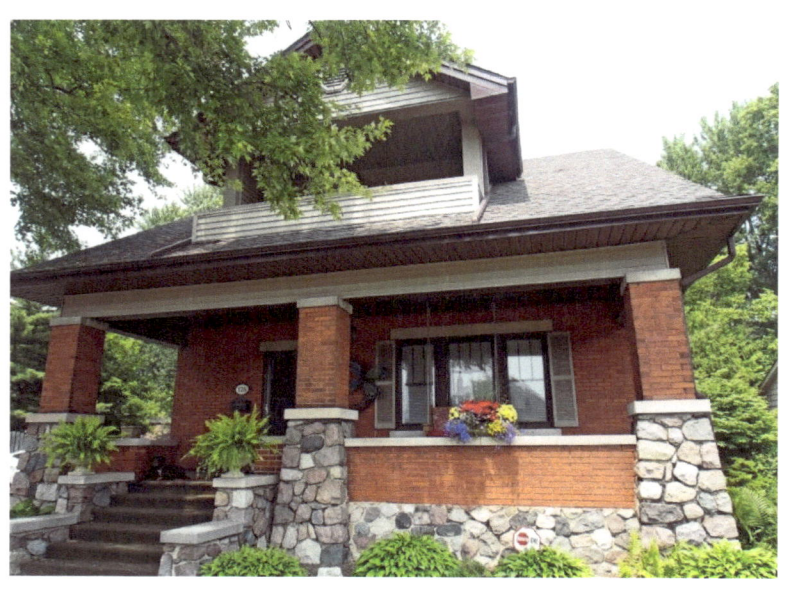

128 Main Street East – Arts and Crafts style

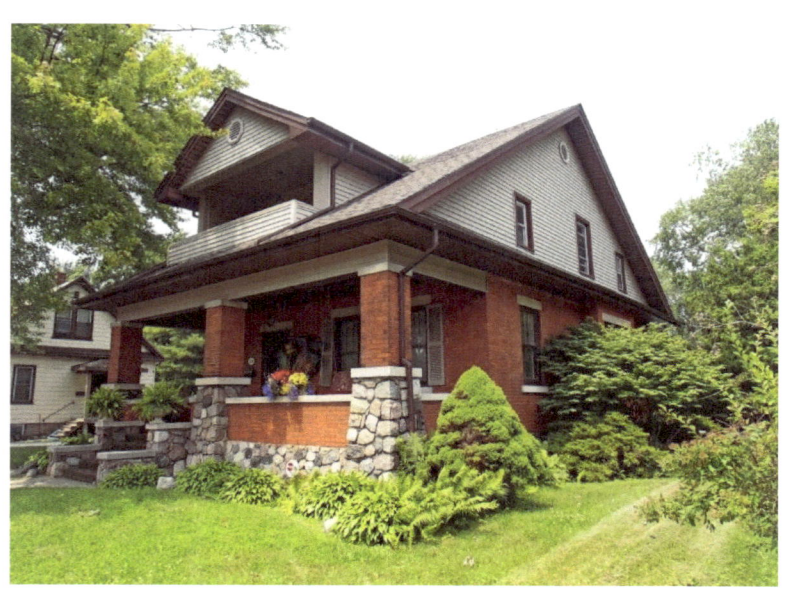

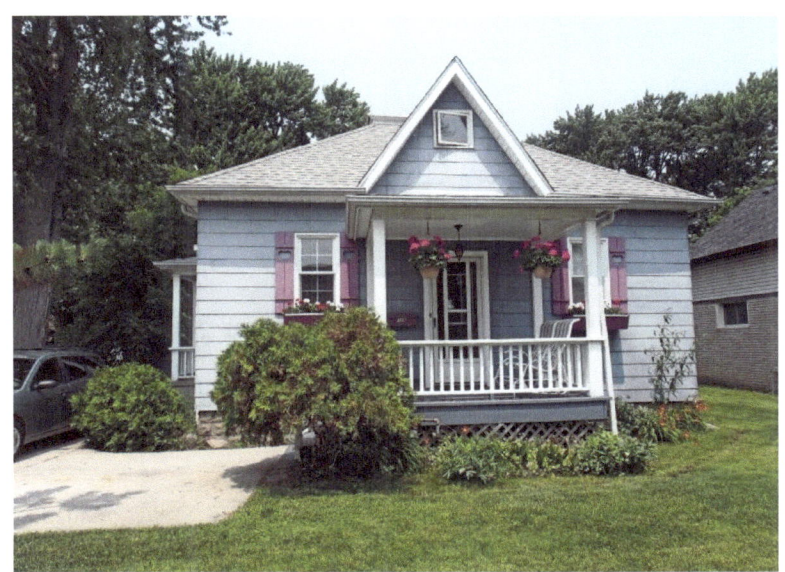

116 Main Street East

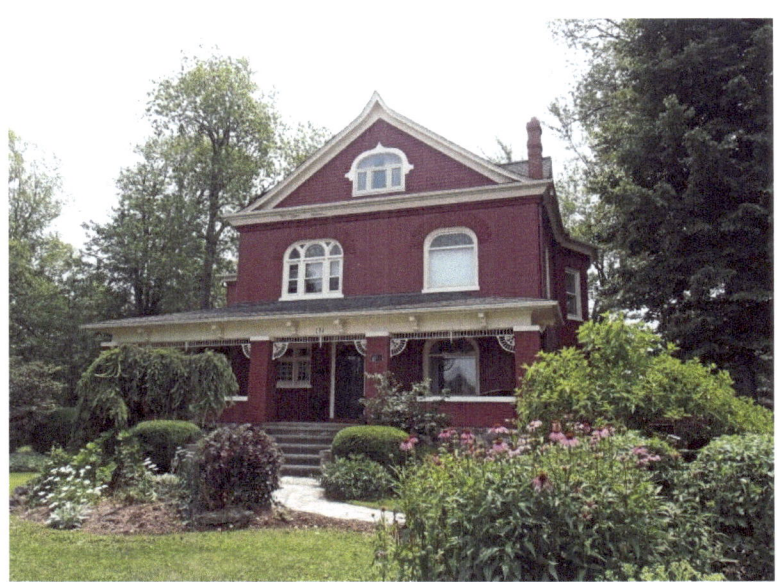

171 Main Street East - built 1902 – Bon Jasperson House – 2½ storey, late Victorian style; raised cut-fieldstone foundation; decorative spindle work on verandah; cornice brackets

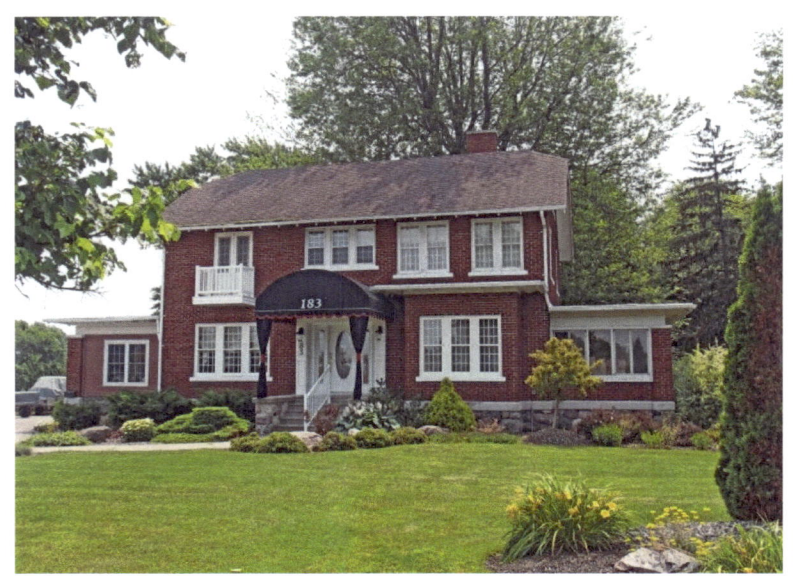

183 Main Street East – Garden Manor Bed and Breakfast
Georgian style built in 1924

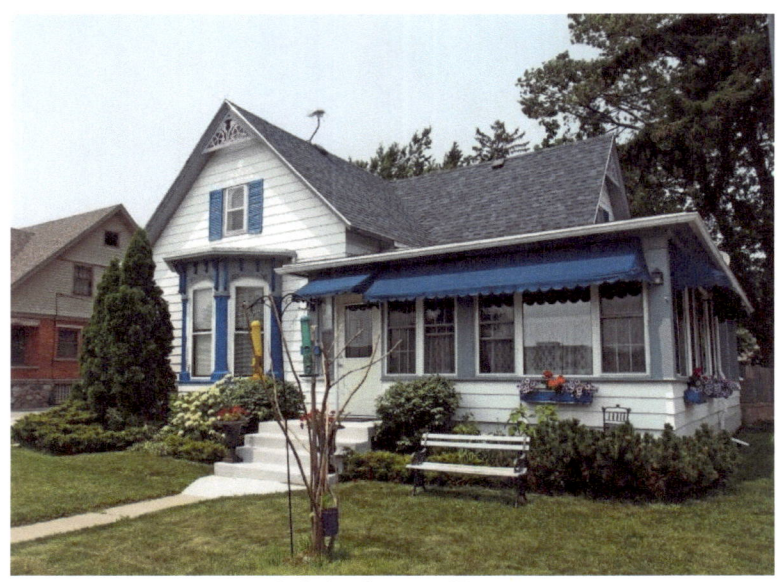

Main Street East

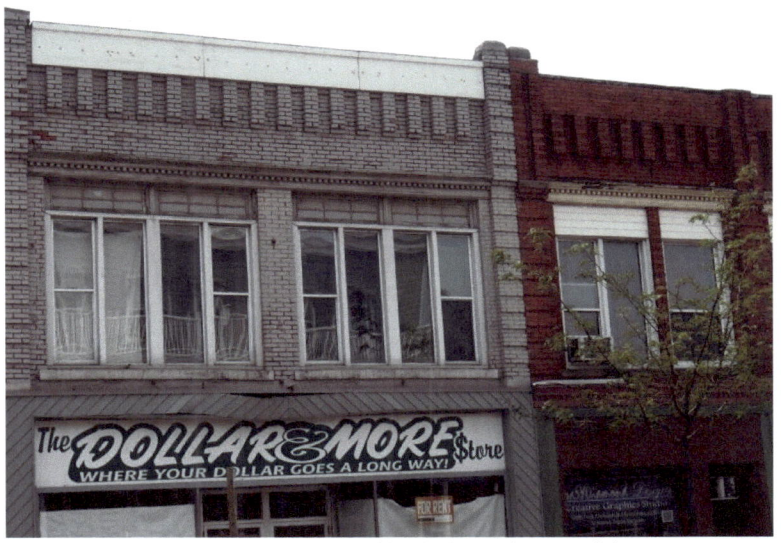

Main Street – bevelled dentil moulding

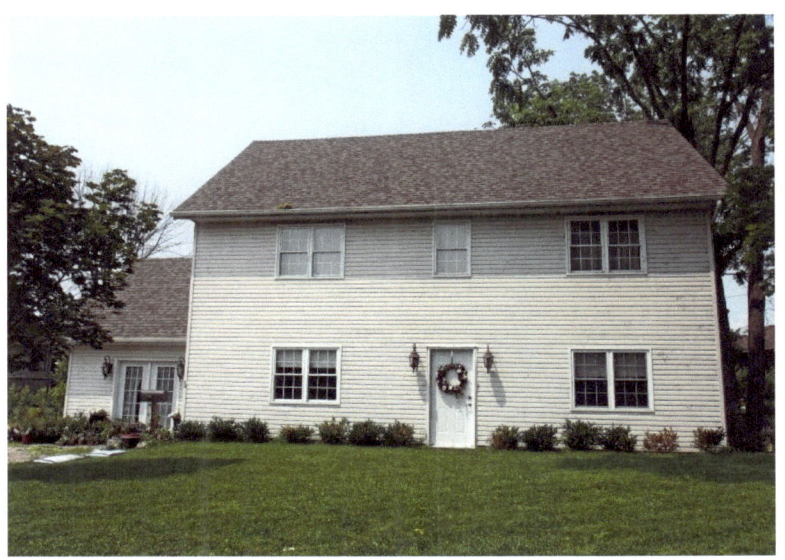

Herrington Street

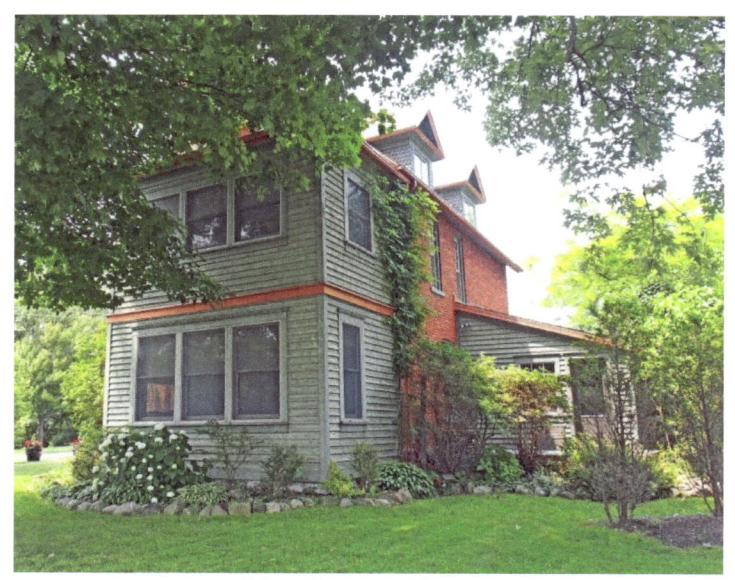

Herrington Street

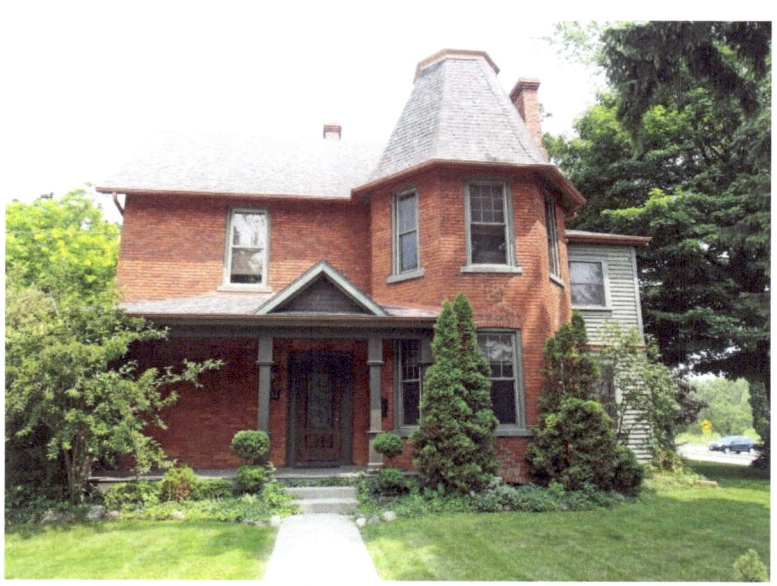

253 Herrington Street - turret

Architectural Terms

Bay Window: A window that projects out from a wall, in a semicircular, rectangular, or polygonal design. Used frequently in Gothic and Victorian designs. Example: 164 Division Street	
Brackets: a decorative or weight-bearing structural element which forms a right angle with one side against a wall and the other under a projecting surface such as an eave or roof. Example: 86 Division Street	
Buttress: a masonry structure built against or projecting from a wall which serves to support or reinforce the wall. In Canadian architecture, they are sometimes used for decoration. Example: 67 Main Street East – St. John de Brebeuf Roman Catholic Church, Page 42	
Capital: The uppermost finish or decoration on a column. A Doric column is characterized by a plain column with no base, a shaft with twenty flutings, and a simple capital with a simple entablature. Example: 59 Division Street, Page 14	
Cobblestone architecture: Refers to the use of cobblestones embedded in mortar as a method for erecting walls on houses and commercial buildings. Example: 78 Division Street, Page 16	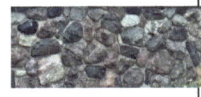

Cornice: originally the wooden overhang of the roof. With the use of stone, brick, iron and steel, the cornice is any projecting shelf at the top of a ceiling or roof. They can be very decorative. Example: 98 Division Street, Page 18	
Dentil Moulding: an even series of rectangles used as ornamental decoration in cornices. Example: Main Street East	
Dormer: (French for "sleep") a gable end window that pierces through the plane of a sloping roof surface to create usable space in the top floor or attic of a building by adding headroom. Example: Division Street, Page 17	
Fretwork: interlaced decorative design resembling a bracket Example: 78 Division Street, Page 16	
Gable: the triangular portion of a wall between the edges of a sloping roof. **Jacobean Gable:** the gable extends above the roofline. Example: 98 Division Street, Page 18	

Hipped Roof: a roof where all sides slope downwards to the walls with no gables. Example: Main Street, Page 40	
Iron Cresting: A decorative ornament along the top of a roof. Iron cresting was popular in the Baroque era and also in Italianate, Victorian, Second Empire and Queen Anne styles of architecture. Example: 111 Division Street	
Keystones and Voussoirs: a voussoir is a wedge-shaped element used in building an arch. A keystone is the central stone that locks all the stones into position, allowing the arch to bear weight. A keystone is often enlarged and embellished. Example: 26 Main Street, Page 37	
Lancet Window: a tall, narrow window with a pointed arch at its top. Example: 67 Main Street East – St. John de Brebeuf Roman Catholic Church, Page 42	
Mansard Roof: This style was popularized by Francois Mansart (1598-1666), an accomplished architect of the French Baroque period and especially fashionable during the Second French Empire (1852-1870). This roof is almost flat on the top section, with two slopes on each of its sides with the lower slope at a steeper angle than the upper and having dormer windows. Example: 76 Main Street East, Page 40	

Pediment: a triangular section above the horizontal structure (entablature), typically supported by columns. The inside of the triangle is called the tympanum. Example: 121 Division Street, Page 21	
Pilaster: a slightly projecting column built into or applied to the face of a wall for additional structural support. Example: 25 Division Street, Page 5	
Quoin: masonry blocks at the corner of a wall, often a decorative feature, usually larger or of a different colour than the rest of the wall. Example: 164 Division Street, Page 24	

Transom Window: the light above the doorway, also called a fanlight. Example: 78 Division Street, Page 16	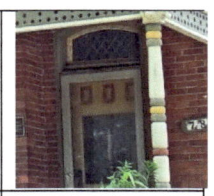
Turret: a small tower that projects from the wall of a building. Example: 253 Herrington Street, Page 50	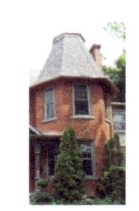
Verge board and Finial: also called bargeboards – hang from the projecting end of a roof and are often elaborately carved and ornamented. **Finial:** ornament added to the top of a gable, pinnacle, canopy or spire – a Gothic element. Example: 90 Main Street East	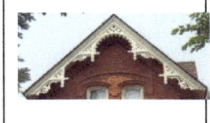
Window Hood: A **hood** is the piece found above window openings, usually of an ornate design, and covers the top third of the opening. Hoods are commonly placed above arched or curved openings on both windows and doors. Example: Main Street East, Annabelle's	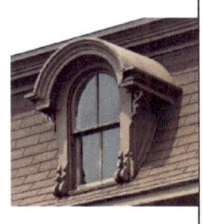

Art Deco, 1910-1940 - The Art Deco Style was developed for the French luxury market after World War I. Art Deco left its mark on everything from lamps and foot stools to purses and hair combs. The style was adopted in Ontario by wealthy and very fashionable patrons who wanted Art Deco detailing to make their buildings look lavish and exotic. Example: 28 Division Street South, Page 7	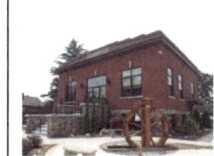
Arts and Crafts: The overlying theme - the house was based on the function of the house. Rooms were oriented to take advantage of the movement of the sun for warmth and light during daylight hours. Side entrances allowed for useable space on the front facade for light or garden use. Arts and Crafts houses have many of these features: wood, stone or stucco siding; low-pitched roof; wide eaves with triangular brackets; exposed roof rafters; porch with thick square or round columns; stone porch supports; exterior chimney made with stone; open floor plans with few hallways; many windows, some with stained or leaded glass; beamed ceilings; dark wood wainscoting and moldings; built-in cabinets, shelves, and seating. Example: Main Street East, Page 41	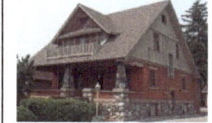

Colonial Revival architecture seeks to revive elements of architectural style of American colonial architecture of the period around the Revolutionary War which drew strongly from Georgian architecture of Great Britain. Architecture from the 18th and early 19th centuries in Ontario includes a wide assortment of detailing and ornament applied to a design centered around the fireplace and the source of water. Structures are typically two stories, have a symmetrical front facade with elaborate front doorways, often with decorative crown pediments, fanlights, and sidelights, symmetrical windows flanking the front entrance, often in pairs or threes, and columned porches. Example: 31 Division Street South, Page 13	
Edwardian, 1900-1930 – This style bridges the ornate and elaborate styles of the Victorian era and the simplified styles of the 20th century. Balanced facades, simple roof lines, dormer windows, large front porches, and smooth brick surfaces are its characteristics. Example: Division Street, Page 10	
Georgian, before 1860 – This style began with the British King Georges in the 18th century. These buildings have balanced facades around a central door, medium-pitched gable roofs, and small paned windows. Example: 183 Main Street East, Page 48	

Gothic Revival, 1830-1890 – These decorative buildings have sharply-pitched gables with highly detailed verge boards, pointed-arch window openings, and dichromatic brickwork. It is a common style in Ontario. Example: 90 Main Street East, Page 45	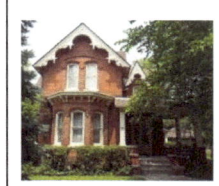
Italianate, 1850-1900 – It has wide-bracketed eaves, belvederes, wrap-around verandahs. Example: 29 Main Street West, Page 36	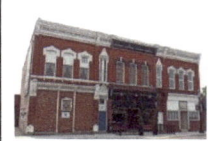
Queen Anne, 1885-1900 – This style is distinguished by an irregular outline featuring a combination of an offset tower, broad gables, projecting two-storey bays, verandahs, multi-sloped roofs, and tall, decorative chimneys. A mixture of brick and wood is common. Windows often have one large single-paned bottom sash and small panes in the upper sash. Example: 98 Main Street West, Page 43	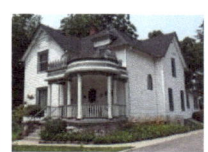
Second Empire, 1860-1880 – The mansard roof is the most noteworthy feature of this style and is evidence of the French origins. Projecting central towers and one or two-storey bays can also be present. Example: 76 Main Street East, Page 39	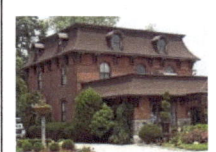

Vernacular/Traditional Mode 1638 - 1950 Influenced but not defined by a particular style, vernacular buildings are made from easily available materials and exhibit local design characteristics. Example: 176 Division Street, Page 26	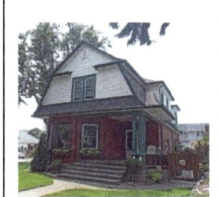
Victorian - In Ontario, a Victorian style building can be seen as any building built between 1840 and 1900 that doesn't fit into any of the other categories. It encompasses a large group of buildings constructed in brick, stone, and timber, using an eclectic mixture of Classical and Gothic motifs. Example: 171 Main Street East, Page 47	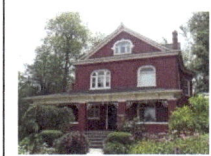
Folk Victorian: square, symmetrical shape, cornice brackets, porches with spindle work. Life was simple before the age of railroads. In the remote parts of North America, families built no-fuss, square or L-shaped houses in the National or Folk style. The rise of industrialization made it easier and more affordable to add decorative details which were mass produced and shipped by railroad across the continent. Example: 189 Division Street, Page 28	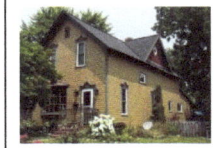

www.ingramcontent.com/pod-product-compliance
Lightning Source LLC
Chambersburg PA
CBHW040852180526
45159CB00001B/399

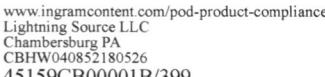